MISUSE OF DRUGS
AND DRUG TRAFFICKING
OFFENCES ACT
(with flowchart)

PATRICK BUCKNELL, MA(Cantab),
Of the Inner Temple, Barrister

and

HAMID GHODSE, MD, PhD, FRCPsych, DPM,
*Professor of Psychiatry of Addiction,
University of London
Consultant Psychiatrist,
St George's and St Thomas's Hospitals, London*

SUPPLEMENT NO. 2 (CUMULATIVE)
Law stated as at 1 January 1988

WATERLOW PUBLISHERS

First published 1988
© P. Bucknell and H. Ghodse 1986, 1988

Waterlow Publishers
Oyez House, PO Box 55
27 Crimscott Street
London SE1 5TS
A division of Hollis Financial and Professional Services PLC

ISBN 0 08 033107 6

Printed in Great Britain by
A. Wheaton & Co Ltd, Exeter, Devon

Publisher's Note

This second (cumulative) supplement contains all matter in the first supplement (with a white cover) published in December 1986 (unless subsequently repealed or rendered otiose), as well as considerable new material. Readers with the first supplement may safely discard it.

The new material covers trends in drug trafficking and abuse, important English and Scottish cases and several new statutory instruments, including the new Crown Court Rules and R.S.C. Order 115 providing the mechanism for handling confiscation orders under the Drug Trafficking Offences Act. The supplement forms a useful guide to the provisions and operation of the Act in its own right, as well as updating the main work.

In the updating notes, matter which amends or expands a paragraph in the main work has the paragraph no. enclosed in square brackets. New paragraphs added to chapters of the main work have their numbers printed in bold type. The new Chapters 14A and 27–33 are set out in the same manner as the main work.

The law is stated at 1 January 1988.

Contents

Table of Cases

(Cases are only included if mentioned for the first time in this or the preceding supplement, or if taken to a further stage, unless marked *, which indicates an additional citation to that in the main text.)

Controlled Drugs

Alphabetical List of Some Contolled Drugs by their Trade Names

Trade Name	Contains	Class	Para.
Amytal	Amylobarbitone	B	3.35
Apisate	Diethylpropion	C	3.19
Benzedrine	Amphetamine	B	3.19
Dexedrine	Amphetamine	B	3.19
DF 118	Dihydrocodeine	B	—
Diconal	Dipipanone	A	3.10
Distalgesic	Dextropropoxyphene	C	—
Doriden	Glutethimide	B	3.35
Durophet	Amphetamine	B	3.19
Equanil	Meprobamate	C	3.35
Fortagesic	Pentazocine	B	3.13
Fortral	Pentazocine	B	3.13
Librium	Chlordiazepoxide	C	3.36
Mandrax	Methaqualone	B	3.35
Medomin	Heptabarbitone	B	3.35
Methedrine	Methylamphetamine	B	3.19
Mogadon	Nitrazepam	C	3.36
Nembutal	Pentobarbitone	C	3.32, 3.35
Palfium	Dextromoramide	A	3.10
Phanodorm	Cyclobarbitone	B	3.35
Physeptone	Methadone	A	3.08
Preludin	Phenmetrazine	B	3.19
Ritalin	Methylphenidate	B	3.19
Seconal	Quinalbarbitone	B	3.35
Sodium amytal	Amylobarbitone	B	3.35
Soneryl	Butobarbitone	B	3.35
Temgesic	Buprenorphine	not controlled	3.14
Tenuate Dospan	Diethylpropion	C	3.19
Tuinal	Quinalbarbitone and amylobarbitone	B	3.35
Valium	Diazepam	C	3.36
Welldorm	Dichloralphenazone	not controlled	3.35

List of Controlled Drugs with their Trade Names

Controlled drugs are listed in the order in which they appear in the schedules to the Misuse of Drugs Regulations 1985 (set out in Appendix IV to this supplement). Where there is a trade name in common use it appears in Column 2. Column 3 indicates where it is likely to be marketed and by which drug company, and Column 4 gives the classification for the purpose of the Misuse of Drugs Act 1971. An asterisk (*) by the name of a drug indicates that it is marketed in the UK.

Chapter 19 of the main work deals with the predecessor to the 1985 Regulations; see also para. 19.02 of this supplement.

(1) *Approved Name*   (2) *Trade Name*   (3) *Where Marketed*   (4) *Class*

Schedule 1 (previously Schedule 4)
(No general exceptions apply and the substances are not marketed.)

Bufotenine			A
Cannabinol			A
Cannabinol derivatives			A
Cannabis and cannabis resin			B
Coca leaf			A
Concentrate of poppy-straw			A
Eticyclidine			A
Lysergamide			A
Lysergide and other N-alkyl derivatives of lysergamide			A
Mescaline			A
Psilocin			A
Raw opium			A
Rolicyclidine			A
Tenocyclidine			A
4-Bromo-2, 5-dimethoxy-α-methylphenethylamine			A
N, N-Diethyltryptamine			A
N, N-Dimethyltryptamine			A
2, 5-Dimethoxy-α, 4-dimethylphenethylamine			A

Schedule 2, para. 1, Regulations 6, 7, 8, 10

Acetorphine			A
*Alfentanil	Rapifen	GB (Janssen)	A
Allyprodine			A
Alphacetylmethadol			A
Alphameprodine			A
Alphamethadol			A
Alphaprodine	Nisentil	USA/Canada (Roche)	A
Anileridine	Leritine	Canada (Fross)	A
Benzethidine			A
Benzylmorphine (3-benzylmorphine)			A
Betacetylmethadol			A
Betameprodine			A
Betamethadol			A

xiv

(1) Approved Name	(2) Trade Name	(3) Where Marketed	(4) Class
Betaprodine			A
Bezitramide	Burgodin	Belgium/ Netherlands (Janssen)	A
Clonitazene			A
*Cocaine	(substance used in many preparations in GB)		A
Desomorphine			A
*Dextromoramide	Palfium	GB (MCP)	A
*Diamorphine	(as 10 mg tabs.)	GB (Roche)	A
Diampromide			A
Diethylthiambutene	(used in veterinary medicine)		A
Difenoxin	Motofen	USA (McNeil)	A
Dihydrocodeinone O-carboxymethyl- oxime	Dicodid	Germany/Switz. (Knoll)	A A
Dihydromorphine			A
Dimenoxadole			A
Dimepheptanol			A
Dimethylthiambutene			A
Dioxphetyl butyrate			A
*Diphenoxylate	Lomotil	GB (Searle)	A
*Dipipanone	Diconal	GB (Calmic)	A
Drotebanol	Metebanyl	Japan	A
Ecgonine	(breakdown product of cocaine)		A
Ethylmethyl- thiambutene			A
Etonitazene			A
Etorphine	(used in veterinary medicine)		A
Etoxeridene			A
*Fentanyl	Sublimaze	GB (Janssen)	A
Furethidine			A
*Glutethimide	Doriden	GB (Ciba)	B
Hydrocodone	(metabolite of codeine phosphate)		A
Hydromorphinol			A
Hydromorphone	Dilaudid	Australia/Germany (Knoll)	A
Hydroxypethidine			A
Isomethadone			A
Ketobemidone	Cliradon	Switz./Germany (Ciba)	A
Lefetamine			B
Levomethorphan			A
Levomoramide			A
Levophenacylmorphan			A
*Levorphanol	Dromoran	GB (Roche)	A
Medicinal opium			A
Metazocine			A

(1) *Approved Name*	(2) *Trade Name*	(3) *Where Marketed*	(4) *Class*
*Methadone	Physeptone	GB (Wellcome)	A
Methadyl acetate			A
Methyldesorphine			A
Methyldihydro-morphine			A
Metopon			A
Morpheridine			A
*Morphine	MST-Continus	GB (Napp)	A
Morphine methobromide			A
Myrophine			A
Nicomorphine	Vilan	Switz. (Synmedic)	A
Noracymethadol			A
Norlevophanol			A
Normethadone	(used as a cough suppressant)		A
Normorphine	(metabolite of morphine)		A
Norpipanone			A
*Oxycodone	Oxycodone suppositories	GB (Roche)	A
Oxymorphone	Numorphan	Canada/USA/SA (End)	A
*Pethidine	(injection and tablets)	GB (Roche)	A
Phenadoxone			A
Phenampromide			A
*Phenazocine	Narphen	GB (Smith & Nephew)	A
Phencyclidine	(widely used in USA as drug of abuse)		A
Phenomorphan			A
*Phenoperidine	Operidine	GB (Janssen)	A
Piminodine			A
*Piritramide	Dipidolor	GB (Janssen)	A
Proheptazine			A
Properidine			A
Racemethorphan			A
Racemoramide			A
Racemorphan			A
Sufentanil	Sufentanil	Belgium (Janssen)	A
Thebacon	Acedicon	Germany/Holland/Belgium (B. Ingelheim)	A
Thebaine			A
Tilidate	Lak	Argentina (Betnabo)	A
	Kitadol	Spain (Lamia)	A
Trimeperidine			A
4-Cyano-2-dimethylamino-4,4-diphenylbutane			A
4-Cyano-1-methyl-4-phenylpiperidine			A
1-Methyl-4-phenylpiperidine-4-carboxylic acid			A
2-Methyl-3-morpholino-1,1-diphenylpropanecarboxylic acid			A
4-Phenylpiperidine-4-carboxylic acid ethyl ester			A

(1) *Approved Name*	(2) *Trade Name*	(3) *Where Marketed*	(4) *Class*

Schedule 2, para. 6

(1)	(2)	(3)	(4)
Acetyldihydrocodeine	Acetylcodone	Belgium (Bios-Coutelier)	B
Amphetamine	Benzedrine	Spain/Denmark/ USA (Smith Kline & French)	B
*Codeine	Bepro Syrup	GB (Farillon)	B
	Diarrest Syrup	GB (Galon)	
	Kaodene Suspension	GB (Crookes)	
	Tercolix Elixir (injections and syrup)	GB (Vestric) GB (Evans)	
*Dextropropoxyphene[4]	Cosalgesic[1]	GB (Cox)	C
	Distalgesic[1]	GB (Dista)	
	Dextrogesic[2]	GB (Clinmed)	
	Dolosan[2]	GB (Lilley)	
	Doloxene[3]		
*Dihydrocodeine	DF 118 (tabs, elixir and injection)	GB (Duncan Flockhart)	B
	Onadox 118 (+aspirin)		
	Paramol 118 (+paracetamol)		
3-ethylmorphine	Renotin	GB (Lane & Stedman)	B
Mecloqualone	Nubarene	France (Diamant)	B
Methaqualone	(marketing in GB discontinued)		B
Methylamphetamine	(marketing in GB discontinued)		B
*Methylphenidate	Ritalin	GB (Ciba)	B
Nicocodine			B
Nicodicodine			B
Norcodeine	(metabolite of codeine)		B
Phenmetrazine	Preludin	USA (B. Ingelheim)	B
*Pholcodine	Copholco Linctus	GB (Norer)	B
	Colpholcoids Pastilles	GB (Norer)	
	Dia-Tuss Diabetic Linctus	GB (Rona)	

---

1 Cosalgesic, Distalgesic contain dextropropoxyphene and paracetamol
2 Dextrogesic, Dolosan contain dextropropoxyphene and aspirin
3 Doloxene contains dextropropoxyphene, aspirin and caffeine
4 Dextropropoxyphene was formerly marketed in GB as Deproval SA, SU-65 and Doloxytal

(1) Approved Name	(2) Trade Name	(3) Where Marketed	(4) Class
*Pholcodine—cont.	Expulin Linctus	GB (Galen)	
	Falcodyl Syrup	GB (Norton; Vestric)	
	Pavacol D Mixture	GB (B. Ingelheim)	
	PEM Linctus	GB (Laveridge)	
	Pholcomed Linctus	GB (Medo)	
	Pholtex Mixture	GB (Riker)	
	Rubelix Syrup	GB (Pharmax)	
	Sancos Linctus	GB (Sandoz)	
	Triocos Syrup	GB (Wander)	
	Triopaed Syrup	GB (Wander)	
	Valledrine Linctus	GB (May & Baker)	
Propiram	Algeril	Netherlands (Bayropharm)	B

Schedule 3, Regulations 6, 7, 9, 10

(1) Approved Name	(2) Trade Name	(3) Where Marketed	(4) Class
Benzphetamine	Didrex	USA (Upjohn)	C
Chlorphentermine	Apsedon	Spain (Lensa)	C
	Pre-Sate	USA (Parke Davis)	
*Diethylpropion	Apisate	GB (Wyeth)	C
	Tenuate Dospan	GB (Merrell)	
Ethchlorvynol	Placidyl	USA/Canada (Abbott)	C
Ethinamate	Valmid	USA (Dista)	C
*Mazindol	Teronac	GB (Wander)	C
Mephentermine	Wyamine	Belgium (Wyeth)	C
*Meprobamate	Equanil	GB (Wyeth)	C
	Meprate	GB (DDSA Pharm.)	
	Milonorm	GB (Farillon)	
	Miltown	GB (Pharmax)	
	Tenavoid (+bendro-fluazide)	GB (Burgess)	
*Methylpheno-barbitone	Prominal	GB (Winthrop)	B
*Methyprylone	Noludor	GB (Roche)	C
*Pentazocine	Fortral	GB (Winthrop)	B
	Fortagesic (+paracetamol)		
Phendimetrazine	Anorex	USA (Dunhall)	C

(1) Approved Name	(2) Trade Name	(3) Where Marketed	(4) Class
*Phentermine	Duromine	GB (Carnegie)	C
	Ionamin	GB (Lipha)	
Pipradrol	Detaril	Italy (ISOM)	C

Schedule 4, Regulations 4, 6, 7, 9, 10

(This new Schedule lists products excepted from prohibition on import, export and, when in the form of a medicinal product, possession. All were brought under control by the Misuse of Drugs Act 1971 (Modification) Order 1985 (S.I. no. 1995), set out in Appendix XV.)

Alprazolam	Xanax	USA (Upjohn)	C
Bromazepam	Lexatin	Spain (Roche)	C
Camazepam	Albego	Belgium (Sintesta)	C
*Chlordiazepoxide	Librium	GB (Roche)	C
	Tropium	GB (DDSA Pharm.)	
*Clobazam	Frisium	GB (Hoechst)	C
*Clonazepam	Rivotril	GB (Roche)	C
*Clorazepic acid	Tranxene (as depot salt)	GB (B. Ingelheim)	C
Clotiazepam	Trecalmo	Germany (Tropen)	C
Cloxazolam	Enadel	Japan (Tropen)	C
Delorazepam			C
*Diazepam	Atensine tablets	GB (Berk)	C
	Diazemuls (injection)	GB (Kabi Vitrium)	
	Evacalm tablets	GB (Unimed)	
	Solis (capsules)	GB (Galen)	
	Tensium tablets	GB (DDSA Pharm.)	
	Valium	GB (Roche)	
	Valrelease S/R	GB (Roche)	
Estazolam	Domnamid	Denmark (Lundbeck)	C
Ethyl loflazepate		France (Clin. Midy)	C
Fludiazepam			C
Fluntitrazepam	Darkene	Netherlands (Sigunta)	C
*Flurazepam	Dalmane	GB (Roche)	C
Halazepam		USA (Schering)	C
Haloxazolam			C
*Ketazolam	Anxon	GB (Beechams)	C
*Loprazolam	Dormonoct	GB (Roussel)	C
*Lorazepam	Ativan	GB (Wyeth)	C
*Lormetazepam	Noctamid	GB (Schering)	C

(1) *Approved Name*	(2) *Trade Name*	(3) *Where Marketed*	(4) *Class*
*Medazepam	Nobrium	GB (Roche)	C
Nimetazepam	Erimin	Japan (Sunitomo)	C
*Nitrazepam	Mogadon	GB (Roche)	C
	Nitrados	GB (Berk)	
	Remnos	GB (DDSA Pharm.)	
	Somnite	GB (Norgine)	
	Surem	GB (Galen)	
Nordazepam	Demadar	Argentina (Volpino)	C
*Oxazepam	Serenid D, Serenid Forte	GB (Wyeth)	C
Oxazolam	Convertal	Argentina (Roemmers)	C
Pinazepam	Domar	Netherlands (Zambeletti)	C
*Prazepam	Centrax	GB (Warner)	C
*Temazepam	Euhypnos Euhypnos Forte	GB (Famitalia) (Carlo Erba)	C
	Nomison	GB (Wyeth)	
Tetrazepam	Myolastan	France (Chin-Comar-Byla)	C
*Triazolam	Halcion	GB (Upjohn)	C

Confiscation Orders under Drug Trafficking Offences Act

KEY TO PROCEDURE

1. X is convicted of a *"drug trafficking offence"* in respect of which proceedings were instituted after 12 January 1987 (section 38(4))—see section 38(1) and para. 28.01.

↓

2. Before sentence the court determines whether X has benefited from *"drug trafficking"*—see section 1 and para. 28.01.

↓

3. The court assesses the value of X's proceeds of drug trafficking—see section 2 and 4(1) and para. 28.04.*

↓

4. The court assesses the amount to be recovered—see section 4(2) and (3) and paragraph 28.02. A certificate may be issued under section 4(2) and *must* be issued if the amount to be recovered is less that the assessed value of proceeds—section 4(3).*

*The court may make assumptions under section 2(2) and (3)—see para. 28.04. The court shall have regard to any statements under section 3—see para. 28.03.

↓

5. The court makes the confiscation order which has effect as if the amount were a fine. The court fixes a period of imprisonment in default of payment having regard to the table in section 6(1)—see section 6 and para. 28.05.

↓

6. The court sentences X on the conviction before it. The court may take account of the confiscation order in making a fine or ordering forfeiture—but not in imposing a period of imprisonment—see sections 1(5) and para. 28.01.

↓

7. X may appeal to the Court of Appeal.

↓

8. X may apply to the *High Court* for a certificate that the property available is inadequate for full satisfaction of the confiscation order—section 14 and para. 31.01.

↓

9. If X is granted such a certificate, he may return to the Crown Court and request a reduction in the amount ordered. The court has a discretion in the amount of the reduction it may order. It must adjust the term of imprisonment in default—section 14(3) and para. 31.01.

Updating Notes on Main Work

The Convention on Psychotropic Substances was ratified by the United [1.09] Kingdom on 24 March 1986. In February 1986 a number of new drugs were included in the schedules to the Convention. Most of them were already controlled but there are eight drugs which have since been brought under control. These are:

cathine
cathinone
fencamfamin
fenethyline
fenproporex
mefenorex
propylhexedrine
pyrovalerone

These are included in S.I. 1986/2230 set out in Appendix III of this supplement.

The Drug Trafficking Offences Act 1986

(The Act is set out in Appendix XVI. See also chapters 27–33 of this **1.19** supplement.)

This legislation results from the visit to the United States by the Home Affairs Select Committee of the House of Commons in 1985. It is also strongly influenced by the report of the Hodgson Committee, *Profits of Crime and their Recovery*, Cambridge Studies in Criminology LII. The principal object is to make provision for confiscatory fines to ensure that no one profits by trafficking in controlled drugs (see para 27.01 of this supplement for definitions). It contains provisions which change substantially and to very great disadvantage the position of a defendant before a court. This is justified by Parliament because of the scale of the threat to society which is presented by increased abuse of dangerous controlled drugs, in particular of heroin and cocaine. The Select Committee has described abuse of drugs as "the most serious peacetime threat to our national well-being".

The Parliamentary Under Secretary of State for the Home Department

1.19   (Mr David Mellor) said in the House of Commons about the Bill (second reading debate, 21 January 1986): "What we are doing is trying to take from other areas of the law, particularly the civil law, things that have worked well, like the Mareva injunctions and the vigorous investigations by the High Court masters. We have tried to ensure that they are put at the service of the criminal law so that we do not repeat the mistake that Parliament made in 1971." (See para 17.05 of the main work.)

The Act leaves intact the existing forfeiture powers under the Customs and Excise Management Act 1979 and the Misuse of Drugs Act 1971. The new scheme is based on confiscation orders which are made in the Crown Court. These are supported by restraint orders and charging orders, made by the High Court, to prevent assets being disposed of before a confiscation order can be made and enforced. Once a confiscation order has been made by the Crown Court the High Court may appoint a receiver and exercise various powers in relation to enforcement and the realisation and application of assets. In addition a confiscation order may be enforced as if it were a fine but subject to enhanced periods of imprisonment up to a maximum of ten years in default (section 6).

A new offence with a maximum penalty of fourteen years' imprisonment is created to deal with persons who assist traffickers to retain their assets (section 24). Provision is made in section 24(3) for protection for persons who disclose their suspicions to the authorities concerning funds in their hands. Such "laundering" is defined as a serious arrestable offence.

The Act applies to property whether it is situated in England and Wales or elsewhere (section 38(3)). Provision is made for enforcing confiscation orders in Scotland and for Orders in Council to be made enforcing in England and Wales corresponding orders made in Northern Ireland and in countries outside the United Kingdom.

Powers additional to those in the Police and Criminal Evidence Act 1984 are provided in relation to drug trafficking. These are sanctioned by a new offence with a maximum penalty of five years' imprisonment for any person who makes any disclosure which is likely to prejudice an investigation (section 31). Drug trafficking offences are made "serious arrestable offences" (see para 16.07 of the main work).

A new summary offence with a maximum penalty of six months' imprisonment is created by insertion of a new section 9A into the Misuse of Drugs Act 1971. This is to deal with the supply of articles which may be used or adapted for the administration of controlled drugs. This was inspired by the practice of some shops in Soho of selling cocaine sniffing kits. It is set out in Appendix III to this supplement.

Drug distribution in body fluids and the interpretation of analytical results

The choice of body fluid for drug analysis depends on a number of **2.08A**
factors that are different for each drug, but the principal consideration
is the distribution of the drug between the body fluids. This distribution
will change with the time the drug has been in the body and the dose.

A drug enters the body via the alimentary canal or respiratory system,
or by injection and circulates in the bloodstream either as the free drug or
attached to a protein. To produce its action in the body (pharmacological
action), the drug must pass from the bloodstream to the body cells and it
is only the free drug, which is not protein-bound, that can enter the cells.
The percentage of a drug bound to protein is a property of the drug, and
can range from none to more than 90% bound. The drug is removed from
the body and its pharmacological action terminated by a number of
processes. Firstly, it can pass from the bloodstream into the urine via the
kidneys. Secondly, it can be combined in the liver with other chemical
compounds to produce water-soluble conjugates that have no pharmacological action and are rapidly removed from the blood into the urine.
Thirdly, it can be chemically altered to produce metabolites which
frequently have no pharmacological action, although with a few drugs
the metabolite may be active. These metabolites circulate in the blood,
and like the parent drug are conjugated in the liver and removed from the
blood into the urine by the kidneys.

The concentration of a drug in the blood at any given time represents
the amount of drug available to the body cells at the time the blood
sample is taken, and will depend on the rates of both absorption and
elimination of the drug from the bloodstream. The time taken for the
blood concentration to decline by 50% is known as the "half-life" of the
drug. Drugs with short half-lives will have blood levels which change
rapidly with time. Hence drug concentrations in blood samples taken at
different times will give very different results, and cannot be related to the
dose without additional information. It has already been noted that the
free non-protein-bound drug passes from the blood to the body cells. In
addition it also enters the saliva. The measurement of drug concentrations in saliva can give an indication of the free level of the drug in the
blood. When a high percentage of the drug is bound to protein, the saliva
level will be very low. The concentration of a drug in urine is very much
higher than in blood or saliva and represents the total quantity of drug
eliminated through the kidneys during the period of time that the urine
specimen was collected. Most of the drug present in the urine will be in
the form of inactive metabolites and conjugates that may be detected for
a long time after all the active drug has disappeared.

Urine samples are preferred for the analysis of drugs of abuse. They

3

2.08A are readily available and the drugs and metabolites are present in relatively high concentration and can therefore be detected for a long period of time after administration. One disadvantage of a urine sample is that some drugs are found only as metabolites which are common to a number of parent drugs; identification of the parent drug may not then be possible. Urine specimens can be easily interfered with and should be collected under supervision. Blood has the advantage that the parent drug can be measured if the sample is collected soon after the drug was taken. Interference with the sample is also more difficult. The dis-

Table: *Drug distribution in blood and urine*

	Blood		Urine	
	Half-life hours	Blood level microgrammes per ml	90% excretion days	Unchanged drug %
CNS Depressants				
Barbiturates:				
Phenobarbitone	100	15	16	25
Butobarbitone	40	7	7	5
Amylobarbitone	24	6	6	1
Chlormethiazole	5	2		5
Benzodiazepines:				
Diazepam	48	1.5	7	
CNS Stimulants				
Amphetamine	12	2	3	3
Methylamphetamine	9	0.02	1.5	43
Cocaine	1	0.5	2	4
Narcotic Analgesics				
Heroin	0.05			nil
Morphine	3	0.05	1	5
Codeine	3	0.2	1	1
Methadone	15	1.0	2	4
LSD	3	0.004		1
Cannabis	30	0.007	12	

Definitions
1. Half-life: Time in hours for the blood level to decrease by 50%.
2. Blood level: Average blood level for a therapeutic dose of drug.
3. 90% excretion: Time in days for 90% of the drug to be excreted in the urine.
4. Unchanged drug: Percentage of the unchanged drug excreted in the urine.

4

advantages are that the drug concentration in blood is lower than urine; **2.08A**
hence the drug cannot be detected for as long. Saliva is not a suitable
fluid, as the drug concentration is usually very low and it is difficult to
obtain sufficient volume of fluid.

The above table gives some indication of the time that drugs can be
detected in blood and urine after a single dose. The figures are only
average values and will vary from patient to patient as well as with the
frequency and dose of the drug. The period for which it is possible to
detect a drug will depend also on the lowest concentration of drug
detectable by the analytical method. As examples it can be seen from the
table that phenobarbitone will be detected for a long time in both blood
and urine as it has a long half-life and high blood concentration. Heroin
is at the other extreme with a very short half-life and undetectable levels
in both blood and urine.

Opiate Agonist–Antagonist Analgesics
The agonist–antagonist opiates are a comparatively new class of drugs,   [3.12]
introduced as the most recent solution to a long-term problem—how to
provide potent analgesia without the attendant problems of abuse and
dependence associated with the 'parent' opiate agonists. The first of these
drugs was N-allylnorcodeine, an opiate antagonist, which was described
in 1915 and was followed a decade later by the synthesis of norcodeine.
Since 1954, when another antagonist, nalorphine, was found to possess
analgesic properties in man without producing psychic dependence or
opiate-like physical dependence, considerable attention has been focussed
on this class of analgesics. These drugs, publicised as non-addictive
substitutes for opiates, have been widely used both as analgesics and for
the treatment of opiate dependence. However, just as drug addiction
cannot be adequately defined in purely medical or scientific terms because
of its essentially social context, so drug abuse does not always follow neat
pharmacological and experimental pathways. It is well known that people
experiment with drugs with different effects and may continue to abuse
those which initially had unpleasant or undesirable effects; they may also
mix drugs with different and often opposing effects. Therefore, to find out
if a particular drug has a potential abuse liability or is currently being
abused, it is not sufficient only to examine its reinforcing properties in
animals or even to search for physical symptoms of withdrawal. It is also
necessary to establish its black market value (if any) and to see how it is
changing hands at street level.

Previous experience with heroin and methadone warns that it will be
difficult to find an opiate analgesic without dependence liability, but the
development of pentazocine in the 1960s, with its blend of agonist and
antagonist properties held out new hope. It has now been prescribed in

5

[13.12] billions of doses for millions of people and its efficacy as an analgesic is well-established. However, the extent to which it, and other similar drugs are abused, remains controversial.

'New' Agonist–Antagonist Analgesics

3.12A   Following the introduction of pentazocine in 1967 (see para. 3.13 *infra*) many other similar drugs have been developed, including cyclazocine, buprenorphine and butorphanol and nalbuphine. There have been scattered reports of seizures, illicit diversion of drugs and of abuse, but there has been no systematic, epidemiological survey to evaluate the extent of any such abuse. The almost complete lack of data is itself worthy of comment: it could mean, for example, that there is very little or no abuse, and hence no reports, or alternatively that no one is carrying out appropriate surveys to detect it. It is tempting, particularly for those with a commercial interest in these drugs, to assume that the former explanation is correct. However, it should never be forgotten that it took decades for the dependence liability and abuse potential of amphetamine and barbiturates to be recognised, but that once the data-gathering survey began, the scale of the problem quickly became apparent. In fairness, it should be added that the possibility (probability) of abuse and dependence on agonist/antagonist drugs has been recognised from the start so that these problems are more likely to be recognised than they were with barbiturates and amphetamine in their early days. It must also be remembered that these drugs have not (yet) achieved full, wide-scale global penetration and that if and when they do, active epidemiological surveying for abuse will be essential.

As a class they have both analgesic and opiate antagonist activity in both animals and humans. While there are some quantitative differences between the different members of this class of drugs, they are qualitatively similar. At equianalgesic doses they all depress respiration to the same degree as morphine. This means, for example, that if 30 milligrams of pentazocine have the same analgesic effect as 10 milligrams of morphine, then they will also depress respiration to the same extent as would 10 milligrams of morphine. Unlike morphine, however, larger doses of the agonist/antagonist analgesics do not cause greater respiratory depression and therefore apnoea (cessation of breathing) never or rarely occurs. With the exception of buprenorphine, their respiratory depressant effects can be reversed by the pure antagonist naloxone, although it requires a higher dose than that needed for opiates. The respiratory depressant effects of buprenorphine are only partially reversed by naloxone. (Naloxone itself has no abuse potential and is considered to be a pure opiate antagonist which is used as a very effective antidote in opiate poisoning, when it is often life-saving).

6

antidotes for opiate poisoning;
agents for treating addicts;
tools in neuroscience;
diagnostic agents for physical dependence;
analgesics of lower abuse potential.

Although all opiate antagonist-analgesics, due to their mood-elevating effects, are candidates for misuse, drugs which do not produce any agonistic effects (e.g. naloxone and naltrexone) have not apparently been abused. Drugs such as butorphanol and nalbuphine, although pharmacologically dependence-producing with a clear-cut reinforcing effect, are relatively new drugs and there are only a few case-reports of abuse. As yet it is probably too early in their "career" for any definitive evidence about their abuse potential. The most widely used opiate-antagonist analgesics, pentazocine and buprenorphine, were introduced into clinical practice as "safe" analgesics with no abuse potential. Case reports of their abuse soon started to appear, but nevertheless it has taken many years to accumulate a substantial number which still represent only certain parts of the world.

It is probably realistic to assume that all psychoactive drugs including opiate antagonist-analgesics possess some dependence-producing liability and that to describe any of them as "safe" drugs, which do not produce dependence, is misleading. In this context safety is only a relative concept, although the opiate antagonist-analgesics are often compared favourably with morphine, for example. It has been suggested that some drugs may be drugs of dependence but not of abuse, either because of unpleasant initial effects or because they do not produce a quick escape from reality, and as yet there is little evidence of widespread abuse of some opiate antagonist drugs. Individual case reports often stress that the patient had previously misused other drugs, implying that an underlying propensity for drug abuse may have been more important than the properties of the drug itself. It follows that the full dependence liability of these drugs may well be exposed if they become frequent drugs of abuse of individuals deliberately exploring their psychic effects. It is important that lessons of pharmaceutical history should not be forgotten—that heroin and cocaine were both used to "cure" morphine dependence and that it took 30 years and 50 years respectively for the dependence-producing potential of amphetamine and barbiturates to be appreciated. Any claims for the lack of abuse liability of any psychoactive substance must be viewed with extreme scepticism.

As far as opiate antagonist–analgesics are concerned, pharmacological theory should not lull doctors into complacency and excessive prescribing.

3.12A   Equally, care should be taken not to over-react to individual and often isolated case reports, but to assess each drug separately on the basis of all the existing evidence which, for many of these drugs, is unfortunately very limited.

Pentazocine

[3.13]   Pentazocine (now controlled—Class B) is a benzomorphan derivative with both opiate agonistic actions and weak antagonistic activity. It is a potent analgesic; a dose of 30 mg is usually as effective an analgesic as 10 mg of morphine, or 75–100 mg of pethidine. In smaller doses it produces essentially the morphine-like effects of euphoria, but with larger doses dysphoria occurs. Chronic use of pentazocine produces physical and psychological dependence and when discontinued an abstinence syndrome occurs. It is available in both oral and powdered forms and is marketed under the trade names Fortral (in UK) and Talwin (in the USA). It was made a controlled drug by the Misuse of Drugs Act 1971 (Modification) Order 1985 (S.I. no. 1995)—see Appendix XV of main work.

Abuse of pentazocine and the magnitude of the problem has varied considerably from country to country. Much of the problem has been with health care personnel, but during the late 1970s and early 80s an epidemic of combined use of pentazocine and the anti-histamine tripelennamine (Ts and Blues) occurred in the USA. A naloxone/pentazocine oral medication is now being marketed. Naloxone does not antagonise pentazocine when taken orally, but does if the tablet is crushed and injected intravenously. This has led to a decrease in the number of reports of abuse of this drug in the US.

Pentazocine was the first drug in this class of compounds to be internationally controlled under Schedule III of the 1971 Psychotropic Convention.

Buprenorphine (not controlled)

[3.14]   Buprenorphine is a semi-synthetic opiate derived from thebaine. Chemically, it is in the family of oripavine derivatives, which are among the most potent opiates known. It is structurally related to the potent antagonist diprenorphine. Buprenorphine is a partial agonist of the morphine type. It has morphine-like analgesic, subjective and physiological effects, producing analgesic and other central nervous system effects that are qualitatively similar to those of morphine. Its analgesic potency is estimated to be 25 to 40 times that of morphine and its subjective and respiratory depressant effects are unequivocally slower in onset, but longer-lasting than those of morphine. It is difficult to antagonise the acute effects with pure antagonists (naloxone).

At the same time, buprenorphine acts like an opiate antagonist. [3.14] Depending on the dose, it produces symptoms of abstinence in patients (addicts) who have been receiving morphine-like drugs for several weeks. This antagonistic potency is equivalent to that of naloxone, but of a longer duration, comparable to that of naltrexone. Administration of buprenorphine to patients already receiving large doses of narcotic drugs should be cautious until the response is established, since its antagonist activity might precipitate an abstinence syndrome in this situation. Buprenorphine has an euphoriant effect and individuals using it report opiate-like effects, although the "rush" or "rapid high" that follows heroin injection does not usually occur. Numerous addicts have reported a generalised feeling of contentment and some prefer it to methadone. Buprenorphine causes physical dependence, but drug withdrawal signs are milder than with opiates and occur only slowly, a week or two after the last dose; they include nausea, vomiting, restlessness, insomnia and diarrhoea.

Misuse of buprenorphine has been reported in West Germany, New Zealand, Australia, UK and some other countries. The therapeutic usefulness of buprenorphine is well recognised in the management of intractable pain post-operatively. Buprenorphine is available as a hydrochloride for parenteral use (not administered by mouth) (1 and 2 ml ampoules contain 0.3 mg buprenorphine hydrochloride/ml) and as sublingual tablets (0.4 mg). Buprenorphine is available in the UK on prescription for the relief of mild to moderate pain and is not currently covered by the Misuse of Drugs Act nor by international conventions.

Butorphanol (not controlled)
Butorphanol has a profile of actions similar to that of pentazocine, but **3.14A** is 30 times more potent. The duration of analgesia is approximately equivalent to morpine (3–4 hours). It was introduced to the UK in 1978, but was only available for parenteral administration and was withdrawn from the market in 1983. In the USA the drug is marketed as butorphanol tartrate (Stadol), a white crystalline substance. The administration of butorphanol to patients already receiving large doses of narcotic drugs should be undertaken with caution until the response is established, because it might precipitate an abstinence syndrome in this situation. A number of individual case reports describing butorphanol dependence and withdrawal as well as butorphanol-precipitated withdrawal have been published.

Meptazinol (not controlled)
Meptazinol is a synthetic opiate agonist/antagonist drug which is **3.14B** effective in the relief of moderate to severe pain. In therapeutic doses it does not appear to induce morphine-like subjective effects in patients or

3.14B addicts, and when administered to opiate addicts, it provokes a mild to moderate withdrawal syndrome. It has been marketed both in oral and injectable form in the UK since 1983, and so far there have been no reports of its abuse or addiction. Meptazinol is not controlled under the Misuse of Drugs Act 1971. It is available for medical use on prescription.

Nalbuphine (not controlled)

3.14C Nalbuphine hydrochloride is a synthetic opiate agonist/antagonist analgesic which is chemically related to both naloxone and oxymorphone. It is used for the relief of moderate to severe pain and for preoperative analgesia as a supplement to surgical anesthesia. Its analgesic potency is essentially equivalent to that of morphine on a ml to mg basis. Chronic administration of nalbuphine produces physical dependence that resembles dependence on pentazocine. Abrupt discontinuation of nalbuphine following prolonged use will be followed by symptoms of opiate withdrawal. Although its abuse potential is less than that of morphine, psychological and physiological dependence and tolerance may follow the abuse or misuse of nalbuphine and cases of dependence upon it have been reported. It is marketed under the trade name Nubain and commonly supplied as an injectable solution for medical use on prescription.

[3.15] There has been an increase in the abuse of cocaine. There is a struggle between Columbian and Bolivian producers for the European Market. A trafficking route through West Africa to Spain and into Western Europe has been developed. If the price were to drop there would be a real danger of amphetamine abusers changing over to cocaine.

[3.16] It has become apparent that abuse is more harmful than had been supposed. Progression from sniffing to injecting to free-basing and smoking "crack" leads to such dependence that abusers cannot easily give up. Obtaining the drug takes precedence over all other interests— even their families.

Crack is easier to produce than free-basing. Cocaine hydrocloride is mixed with baking powder and water to form a paste. This is heated in a frying pan or microwave oven. Sometimes ammonia or amphetamine is included in the paste. The name "crack" is derived from the sound it makes as it is heated. Crack is sold as granules in small phials or sealed plastic bags. The granules are smoked in a pipe. As the fumes are inhaled there is an immediate and intense feeling of euphoria as a high concentration of cocaine reaches the brain. This "high" may last about five minutes and it may be followed by depression and irritability. This method of ingesting cocaine leads almost immediately to dependence. The abuse of crack is widespread in the United States of America. It is

10

likely to be trafficked in the United Kingdom in the near future. It is [3.16]
already manufactured by abusers themselves.

The word "dexamphetamine" has been deleted from Schedule 2 to the [3.19]
Misuse of Drugs Regulations by S.I. 1985/1995 following the decision in
R v Watts (1984) 79 Cr.App.R. 127 that the word "amphetamine"
embraces stereoisomers such as dexamphetamine and laevoamphetamine.
   Amphetamines are second only to cannabis in the volume of abuse in
the United Kingdom. They may be described as the poor man's cocaine.
In powder form they are "snorted" or injected. Injection carries with it
the same danger of infection as injection of opiates. They are manufactured illicitly on an increasing scale within the United Kingdom. The
base chemicals are readily available from wholesalers. There have been
suggestions that the base chemicals should themselves be controlled.

Some effects of amphetamine abuse, such as depression and inability to [3.20]
sleep, are not always associated by the user with the taking of the drug a
day or two before. These drugs can cause dependence and distressing
psychological malaises. It may be that the time is near for them to be re-
classified as Class A although, of course, they are already included in
Class A when in the form of a preparation designed for administration by
injection (para (6) of Part 1 of Schedule 2).

Seizures in the form of impregnated paper squares and of micro-dots [3.23]
indicate that LSD may once again be the subject of manufacture in the
United Kingdom. It is possible that the drug may be regaining the
popularity it enjoyed before Operation Julie destroyed the London and
Welsh laboratories in 1977.

Benzodiazepines were added to Class C by S.I. 1985/1995. A number of [3.36]
drugs sharing the characteristics of diazepam (Valium) are included in
Schedule 2 but they are excepted from controls on importation, export-
ation and, when in the form of a medicinal product, possession, by
Schedule 4 to the Misuse of Drugs Regulations (S.I. 1985/2066). (See
Appendix IV *post.*) "Medicinal product" has the same meaning as in the
Medicines Act 1968.
   Benzodiazepines have become a problem to the extent that Drug
Addiction Treatment Units have to initiate withdrawal programmes for
patients who are physically dependent on these drugs.

"Designer drugs" or analogues of narcotic drugs—Class A

The Home Office has acted to control "designer drugs" before they arrive **3.40**
on the black market in the United Kingdom by making S.I. 1986/2230

3.40   (Appendix III). This order includes in Class A carfentanil and lofentanil, which are analogues of fentanyl, and any other analogues of fentanyl or of pethidine which may appear as drugs of abuse.

The term was originally coined to refer to the ability of chemists in illicit laboratories to produce drugs designed to fit the tastes of individual clients. It is now widely used to refer to clandestinely produced substances which are chemically and pharmacologically similar to controlled drugs but which are not themselves controlled. Designer drugs of the eighties include fentanyl analogues and pethidine (known as meperidine in the U.S.A.) analogues. Fentanyls are a class of very potent narcotic analgesics which, although quite different from opiates and opioids in terms of chemical structure, nevertheless possess all the pharmacological and toxicological actions of the classical narcotics.

Fentanyl itself is widely used as an anaesthetic and a post-surgical analgesic, and some of its derivatives currently in therapeutic use are as much as 6,000 times as potent as morphine. With some changes in fentanyl's molecular structure a substance has been produced with a heroin-like "high" but which is 250 time more potent than heroin. One gram of the drug can produce 50,000 doses and a couple of milligrams of the "designer" version may be lethal.

Two pethidine analogues have been identified—MPPP, which is up to 30 times as potent as pethidine, and PEPAP, up to 70 times. During illicit manufacture it is common for neurotoxic by-products to be formed which cause an irreversible neurological condition resembling Parkinson's syndrome with muscular rigidity, tremor, and slowness of movement and speech.

There are considerable technical problems in detecting and accurately identifying drugs in body fluids when they are so powerful that only microscopic doses are involved. There are also real problems in coping with medical emergencies resulting from the abuse of unique and very unfamiliar drugs.

Analogues of fentanyl and pethidine have not yet been reported as drugs of abuse in the United Kingdom.

3.41   *MDMA (Ecstasy)—Class A*
MDMA is an analogue of methamphetamine. This and similar analogues of amphetamine known as MDA, DMA, PMA, TMA and MMDA, and BDMPEA, an analogue of phenethylamine, were added to what is now Schedule 1 of the Misuse of Drugs Regulations (as paragraphs 1(b) and (c)) by S.I. 1977/1243. Thanks to the foresight of the Advisory Council these substances were already controlled before they had begun to appear as drugs of abuse in the United Kingdom.

A substance offered as "Ecstasy" is likely to be 3, 4-methylenedioxy-   **3.41**
methamphetamine. The exact molecular make-up of the drug will depend
on the exigencies of illicit manufacture.

MDMA is taken by mouth. It produces an increased level of sensory
perception and varying levels of intoxication. The intoxication may
consist either of euphoria or fright accompanied by sensory distortions,
hallucinations, nausea, flushing, increased blood pressure, enlargement of
pupils, reduction in balance and co-ordination. Larger doses may result
in muscular rigidity or tremors followed by convulsions and death. Trials
with primates indicate that abuse of MDMA is likely to lead to dependence.

MDMA was first developed in Germany in 1914 but was never
marketed. Illicit use in the United States of America was detected in the
1970s. It is becoming available in the United Kingdom in the form of
white powder, tablets and capsules illicitly imported from America.

Schedule 1 is now Schedule 5 of the 1985 Regulations.   [5.01]

In *R v Ciappara* [1988] Crim.L.R. 172 customs officers intercepted a letter   [5.03]
containing cocaine. They repacked it with baking powder and delivered it
to the appellant. The appellant was unaware of the importation until it
had been completed. The Court of Appeal held that Ciappara was rightly
convicted of being knowingly concerned in the fraudulent evasion of the
prohibition of importing controlled drugs. There was nothing in section
170(2) which required the activities of the person "knowingly concerned"
to be undertaken before the evasion or attempted evasion of the prohibition.

Knowledge

In the appeal of *Shivpuri* (1986) 2 W.L.R. 988 H.L. Lord Bridge said that   [5.04]
if section 170 of the 1979 Act created three separate offences according to
whether the goods were Class A, Class B or Class C and if each of the
offences involved proof of a different element as part of the *actus reus,*
then it was argued that the word "knowingly" connoted a corresponding
mens rea – knowledge of the importation of goods in the appropriate
category. It that argument was right the task of the prosecution would in
many cases be rendered virtually impossible. He then went on to consider
section 28(3) of the Misuse of Drugs Act 1971 (see para 14.01 of the main
work) and to wonder why it had not been applied to importation
offences. He concluded:

> "The only possible explanation was that the 1971 Act had been drafted on
> the footing that *R v Hussain* made any such provision unnecessary; it

established that the only *mens rea* necessary for proof of any such offence was knowledge that the goods were subject to a prohibition on importation.

R v Hussain had effectively been adopted and endorsed by the legislature and thus remained good law".

(*Hussain* concerned the importation of cannabis in September 1968, when the maximum penalty for importation was ten years, whereas the maximum penalty for importation of other prohibited goods varied but for most goods was two years. *Hennessey* also concerned, *inter alia,* the importation of cannabis in February 1976 and the alleged belief of an appellant that he was bringing back blue films. The maximum penalty for importing Class A and Class B drugs such as cannabis was then fourteen years and for Class C drugs five years, whereas the maximum penalty for importing prohibited goods such as pornography was two years).

It seemed therefore that Lord Scarman's obiter dicta in *Taaffe* could be forgotten but attempts to circumvent *Hussain* and *Hennessey* were launched in two appeals by importers of drugs who had pleaded guilty on the basis that they had mistakenly believed that they were importing pornography. These were the appeals of *R v Ellis* and *R v Street and Smith* (1987) 84 Cr.App.R. 235 heard by a Court presided over by Connor L.J. The Court of Appeal was not moved by the argument that Lord Bridge's conclusions concerning *Hussain* were *obiter dicta.* It held that it was bound by the decision in *Hussain* and *Hennessey* and dismissed the appeals. The following question was certified under section 33 of the Criminal Appeal Act 1968 but leave to appeal to the House of Lords was refused:

"Does a person commit the offence of being knowingly concerned in the fraudulent evasion of prohibition on the importation of goods, contrary to section 170(2) of the Customs and Excise (Management) Act 1979, where he believed that he was evading a prohibition upon the importation of goods arising under one enactment, but in fact had imported goods the importation of which is prohibited under another enactment; e.g. where he believed that he was importing obscene or indecent material but in fact had imported a controlled drug?"

The Court of Appeal refused to certify the following question:

"Does a person commit the offence of being knowingly concerned in the fraudulent evasion of a prohibition on the importation of controlled drugs, contrary to section 170(2) of the Customs and Excise (Management) Act 1979, where he believed that he was evading the prohibition upon the importation of controlled drugs arising under section 3 of the Misuse of Drugs Act 1971 and believed that he was importing controlled drugs of one Class, but had in fact imported controlled drugs of another Class: e.g. where he believed that he was importing drugs of Class A but in fact had imported drugs of Class C?"

Until and unless the position is reconsidered by the House of Lords, the [5.04] decision in *Hussain* (and *Hennessey*) remains the law.

The difficulty in deciding the proper sentence for an importer who is liable to a maximum of life imprisonment for importing heroin whereas he claims he believed he was importing blue films (two years) is unresolved. The judge will have to hear evidence and make up his own mind (see *R v Newton* and para 17.03 post). One need not waste much sympathy on anyone who is prepared to smuggle goods without examining them.

The Court of Appeal had to consider whether circumstantial evidence [5.05] was too tenuous to justify convictions on two counts of importing heroin and cannabis in the appeals of *Van Thoor and Pijpenseel* (23 May 1986— unreported). The evidence was: (1) various packets of heroin and of cannabis were found concealed on a vessel when it docked at Liverpool; (2) the vessel had come from Bombay where drugs are frequently placed on board ships; (3) Van Thoor was in Bombay and flew from Bombay airport shortly before the vessel sailed; (4) a man called "Kutty" spent time on the ship at Bombay; (5) both defendants obtained new passports during the currency of their old ones; (6) both defendants, who were living in Holland on social security, flew to Liverpool on 12 April 1984 having booked return flights on 13 April; (7) both defendants went to the docks and Pijpenseel went on board asking for "Kutty"; (8) Pijpenseel had £450 and Van Thoor had £4,000. The defence unsuccessfully submitted that this did not add up to sufficient evidence. This defence was repeated in the Court of Appeal together with arguments based on the fact that there were separate counts for the heroin and the cannabis. In rejecting the appeal the Court cited *R v Hussain* [1969] 2 Q.B. 567 and *R v Shivpuri* [1986] 2 W.L.R. 988 and held that it was not necessary for the prosecution to prove that all the goods were part of the same consignment. The prosecution had to prove the presence of drugs on the ship and that the appellants knew that "what was on foot" was the evasion of the prohibition on the importation of controlled drugs. It would be quite unrealistic to impose on the prosecution the burden of proving specific knowledge of specific packages.

See also cases discussed in para. 10.05 of main work and *R v Hughes* [5.11] (1985) 81 Cr.App.R. 345 discussed in this supplement at 10.05 *post*.

A conviction in Thailand for possessing drugs does not constitute *autrefois* [5.14] *convict* in relation to a charge of conspiring to import the same drugs into the U.K.: *R v Lavercombe*, C.A. 7 March 1988 (unreported).

15

[5.15]   The House of Lords upheld the conviction of *Shivpuri* – The Times 16 May 1986, [1986] 2 W.L.R. 988. They held that *Anderton v Ryan* was wrongly decided.

On the facts of *Shivpuri* Lord Bridge said:

"The certified question depended on the true construction of the Criminal Attempts Act 1981.

The first question to be asked was whether the appellant intended to receive and store (harbour) and in due course pass on to third parties (deal with) packages of heroin or cannabis which he knew had been smuggled into England from India. The answer was that he did.

Next, did he in relation to each offence, do an act which was more than merely preparatory to the commission of the offence?

The act relied on in relation to harbouring was the receipt and retention of the packages: in relation to dealing, it was meeting the intended recipient.

In each case the act was clearly more than preparatory to the commission of the intended offence; it was not and could not be more than merely preparatory to the commission of the actual offence, because the facts were such that it was impossible.

Did the 'act which is more than merely preparatory to the commission of the offence' in section 1(1) (the *actus reus* of the statutory offence of attempt) require any more than an act which was more than merely preparatory to the commission of the offence which the defendant intended to commit?

Section 1(2) indicated a negative answer; if it were otherwise, whenever the facts were such that the commission of the actual offence was impossible, it would be impossible to prove an act more than merely preparatory to the commission of that offence and subsections (1) and (2) would contradict each other.

The appellant was, on that analysis, rightly convicted."

[6.13]   See now section 68 and Schedule 3 to the Police and Criminal Evidence Act 1984 (set out in Appendix IX to this supplement).

[6.14]   The appeal of *Warwick John Cooper* (1986) 82 Cr.App.R. 74 turned upon the use made by the prosecution of two letters written by his wife. Cannabis was found in a television set. Customs officers replaced the cannabis and eventually delivered the television set to the appellant who carried it into his room. When Customs officers entered the room they found on a table close to the television two letters signed in the names of the appellant and his wife. The letters contained references to cannabis. They were put in evidence as part of the case for the prosecution and the jury had copies of them. In evidence the appellant claimed that he did not know that his wife had written them and he was unaware of their contents. His wife was not called as a witness. It appears to have been accepted that they were, in fact, written by the wife and that the signature in his name was not written by him.

The judgment of the court (Mr Justice Leonard) was: [6.14]

". . . the proper procedure would have been for the prosecution to prove the finding of the letters and the place where they were found as part of their case in order to give notice to the defence of the use which might eventually be made of those letters. But at that stage there should have been no indication of the contents of the letters to the jury. Then at an appropriate stage in the Crown's cross-examination of the appellant, provided of course he gave evidence, as in this case he did, the letters should have been placed before the appellant and he should have been asked whether he was aware of their contents. If he said he was aware of their contents he should have been asked about the passages to which we have referred suggesting that there had, at any rate in the past, been a shortage of drugs in the household."

The effect of the judgment is that, in the absence of any admission concerning documents written by someone other than a defendant, their contents are hearsay and should not be revealed to the jury. The judgment does not make clear why, if letters are on a table close to a suspect in his room and apparently bear his signature, the jury cannot assume that he is responsible for their contents, but it may be that the facts are not fully set out in the judgment.

The case of *R v Madden* [1986] Crim.L.R. 804 also turned upon the use of letters. A trunk containing cannabis was delivered to the appellant's home. In order to prove knowledge, letters found in her flat and written by her husband more than a year before were admitted. These letters referred to cannabis and to smuggling. The appellant had agreed that she realised that they referred to cannabis and its importation. It was held by the Court of Appeal that the letters were admissible to rebut the appellant's defence that the cannabis was unsolicited. The still unreported decisions of *Thrussel* (C.A. 30 November 1981) and *Alexiou* (C.A. 14 November 1983) were followed (see this para. of main work). These two decisions are frequently cited by the Court of Appeal.

The application of *Ali Mustafa* for leave to appeal (Court of Appeal, 17 July 1986, unreported) raised two issues. The first was the relevance of an admission that he had made a diversion on his way out to Pakistan to get heroin for his personal use. The second concerned the question of whether it was oppressive to inflict a long interview on a detainee suffering from withdrawal symptoms.

The Crown's case was that the applicant had driven to Pakistan in order to obtain a quantity of heroin to bring back to England. Various passages in his interviews where he mentioned his addiction to heroin were edited out but a passage concerning a diversion of 150 miles to get heroin because he was sick was left to the jury. The Court of Appeal held that this was a piece of evidence to show that here was a person going

[6.14]   way off course in search of heroin, a matter that could properly be placed
          before the jury in support of the prosecution case that this was not an
          innocent journey but a criminal one. The applicant was interviewed when
          he was suffering from withdrawal symptoms. He was seen by a doctor
          who prescribed a sedative and passed him as fit for interview. He was
          interviewed for two hours on the day of arrest. The next day he was again
          seen by the doctor and an interview began at 12.50 p.m. At 1.10 p.m. the
          interviewing officer suspended the interview because of the condition of
          the applicant. The interview began again at 2.35 p.m., the doctor saw him
          again at 3.00 p.m. and the interview continued with the defendant lying
          down until 5.00 p.m., when the applicant was too sleepy to continue. The
          Court of Appeal held that "oppressive" in these circumstances means
          that the applicant was in such a condition that any confession he might
          make could be thought to be due to pressures upon him because of his
          medical condition. It was a matter for the discretion of the trial judge
          who had heard evidence from the doctor who had three times examined
          the applicant. There was no evidence to this effect from the applicant. He
          had given rational answers throughout the interview and asserted that he
          was fit to be interviewed. The learned judge could have come to no other
          conclusion but that the interviews could rightly be admitted.

          The unreported decision in *Willis* (C.A. 29 January 1979; see this para.
          in main work) was followed in *R v Bagga* (below) and in *R v de los Santos*
          (para. 14A.05 *post*).

Corroboration

Where a courier gives evidence for the the prosecution against the
organiser of the importation, it was held in *R v Hills* [1987] Crim.L.R. 567
that the jury must be warned of the necessity to look for corroboration of
his evidence. Corroboration can be provided by a combination of pieces
of circumstantial evidence, each innocuous on its own. It is important to
consider:

          (1) what the real issues are;

          (2) what the evidence put forward as corroboration does in fact prove;
and

          (3) whether that evidence comes from a source independent of the
accomplice.

          In *R v Bagga*, C.A. 21 May 1986 (unreported) the appellant had been
convicted of being knowingly concerned in the importation of 12.313
kilograms of heroin. The courier and her husband had given evidence
against him and one of the questions arising on the appeal concerned the
issue of corroboraton. The facts that the appellant bought the airline
ticket for the courier and took her to the aerodrome and met her on her

18

return, it was agreed, were undoubtedly capable of amounting to corrobor-   [6.1<
ation. So was the finding of a receipt relating to a suitcase the key of
which the courier had with her which would not open the suitcase she was
carrying—this was to be a concocted defence for her—and the fact that
the appellant had to withdraw from a house purchase after the seizure
of the drugs. What the appellant complained of was the admission of
evidence concerning scales and a briefcase containing plastic bags and
traces of heroin at his home. The Court of Appeal again followed its
decision in *R v Willis* (see this para. in the main work). Evidence of the
prior handling of heroin could not be admissible to show a propensity to
deal in heroin, but the Court had to look to see what was the defence
which the evidence might rebut.

> "It was clear that the appellant was asserting that his going to the aero-
> drome to meet the courier was innocent and that he had no knowledge of
> the heroin. It was accordingly open to the prosecution to invite the jury to
> consider whether the evidence of prior unexplained handling of heroin by
> the appellant destroyed his defence of innocent and ignorant presence."

R v Uxbridge Justices ex parte Sofaer and others (1986) The Times 4
December concerned a case in which aircraft parts seized by the Customs
were destroyed before committal proceedings had commenced. Photo-
graphs had been taken. The divisional Court held that although it was
desirable that exhibits should be preserved there was no overriding duty
on the prosecution provided that adequate secondary evidence was available. *R v Lushington ex parte Otto* [1894] 1 Q.B. 430 had stated the
principle too widely.

Conspiracy/obtaining property by deception   6.1

In the case of *R v Bellman* (1988) 86 Cr.App.R. 40 the Crown was unable
to determine whether the appellant had been selling drugs which he had
no prospect of importing or he had in fact been part of a conspiracy to
import. Accordingly he was indicted with obtaining property by
deception and conspiracy to import as alternatives. The Court of Appeal
held that the Crown should have been put to their election at the close of
their case. The counts were mutually destructive.

A large number of the provisions of the Police and Criminal Evidence   [7.0(
Act 1984 were applied to the Customs and Excise with effect from 1
January 1986 by the Police and Criminal Evidence Act 1984 (Application
to Customs and Excise) Order 1985. The order is set out in Appendix IX
to this supplement. See also section 32(4) of the Drug Trafficking
Offences Act 1986 also set out in that appendix.

Drug trafficking offences are made serious arrestable offences by

[7.00]   section 36 of the Drug Trafficking Offences Act 1986. This section only specifies substantive offences—it does not include conspiracy, aiding and abetting or attempt. Special provisions for delay in notifying an arrest etc. are provided by section 32. Both these sections are set out in Appendix IX to this supplement.

[8.01]   Offences connected with the importation and exportation of controlled drugs are specified in Part III of Schedule I to the Criminal Justice Act 1982. They are "excluded offences" so that offenders are not eligible for early release under section 32 of that Act.

The Home Secretary announced in 1983 that parole will be withheld from prisoners serving five years' imprisonment or longer for offences of drug trafficking. His power to adopt such a policy was upheld by the House of Lords in re Findlay and others [1986] Crim.L.R. 154; [1986] A.C. 318.

[8.04]   In R v Ghandi [1987] Crim.L.R. 205 the appellant, who was arrested in possession of a holdall containing 9.83 kilograms of heroin, pleaded guilty and was called as a witness for the Crown. From the beginning he had always claimed that he believed that he was importing cannabis. His accomplice was convicted. Whilst the jury was considering its verdict the trial judge tried the issue of the appellant's belief and the appellant gave evidence. Having put the appellant forward to the jury as a witness of truth the prosecution felt inhibited against cross-examining him but the judge nevertheless disbelieved his evidence and sentenced him on the basis that he knew that he was importing heroin. It was held that the judge was entitled to reach the decision which he did. In the view of the Court, in a case where the Crown called the defendant as a witness, the trial of an issue such as this should be postponed until the trial of the co-defendant had been concluded. Even if the Crown felt unable to advance any evidential challenge to the version of events given by the accused, counsel for the prosecution should still consider to what extent he could assist the Court by exploring in cross-examination any feature of the accused's story which required cross-examination. The sentence was reduced from eight years to seven years so as to give sufficient credit for his evidence for the prosecution.

A discount for assisting the police may be as much as half the maximum sentence: R v King (1986) 82 Cr.App.R. 210.

On the appeal of Bilinski (1988) 86 Cr.App.R. 146 the Court of Appeal held that although it is irrelevant to conviction that a man believed he is importing cannabis when in fact he is importing heroin, it is relevant to punishment. Considering the decision in Ghandi, the Lord Chief Justice said:

"Where the defendant's story is manifestly false the judge is entitled to [8.04]
reject it out of hand without hearing evidence . . . . It may no doubt be
temping for those who are caught smuggling heroin to say that they
thought it was only cannabis. If such an assertion is persisted in before the
court of trial and is plainly incredible, the judge will be justified in declining
to hear evidence on the matter . . . . If the story is truly absurd it is a waste
of time to call evidence which can only repeat the absurdity."

R v Mackenzie (1985) 7 Cr.App.R.(S) 441 was not approved. (See also *R
v Ogunti* (1987) Crim.L.R. 836.)

Some sentences for importing which have been before the Court of Appeal

Drug and quantity	Value or remarks	Sentence	Reported
Cannabis 800 kg	£1 million	10 years	(1986) 8 Cr.App.R.(S) 472
Cannabis 30 kg	£90,000	6 years	(1987) 9 Cr.App.R.(S) 173
Cocaine 12 kg	£2 million	12 years	(1987) 9 Cr.App.R.(S) 91
Cocaine 2.95 kg	£472,000	10 years	(1986) 8 Cr.App.R.(S) 33
Cocaine 881 g	£140,000	9 years	(1986) 8 Cr.App.R.(S) 213
Cocaine 177 g	£26,000	6 years	(1986) 8 Cr.App.R.(S) 228
Cocaine 98 g	£15,000	6 years	(1987) 9 Cr.App.R.(S) 52
Heroin 9.33 kg	(gave evidence for prosecution)	7 years	[1987] Crim.L.R. 205
Heroin 3.03 kg	*Bilinski* (see above)	8 years	[1987] Crim.L.R. 782
Heroin 1.99 kg	£300,000	10 years	[1987] Crim.L.R. 839

(See para. 17.03 *infra* for sentences for production, supply and possession.)
As to value see *Patel* [1987] Crim.L.R. 839 and para. 11.10 *post*.

As to destruction of seized goods required by the defence as exhibits at [8.05]
the trial, see *R v Uxbridge Justices ex parte Sofaer* (para. 6.14 *ante*).

The Queen's Bench Division confirmed in *re Chotipanang* The Times 28 [8.11]
March 1986 that the offence of fraudulent evasion of a prohibition in
relation to controlled drugs is an offence in respect of "any enactment for
the time being in force relating to dangerous drugs" and so included in
the list of crimes in Schedule 1 of the Extradition Act 1870.

As to proof of and challenge to Orders in Council see Chapter 18 *post*. [9.01]

9.03]   The *ratio decidendi* in the case of *Stevens* was applied by the Court of Appeal in *R v Cunliffe* [1986] Crim.L.R. 547 to a collection of dried psilocybin mushrooms. It was held that it was open to the jury to conclude that the appellant had subjected the picked mushrooms to a process of drying that involved an act of preparation for future use.

The decisions in *Stevens* and in *Cunliffe* were followed in *R v Walker* [1987] Crim.L.R. 565, which concerned a container holding 1,000–2,000 dried psilocybin mushrooms. The Court of Appeal said that the judge must direct the jury that there must be a preparation and that they must be satisfied that it was a preparation containing psilocybin. The word "preparation" must be given its ordinary and natural meaning. The Court declined to express any view as to whether picking the mushrooms could constitute preparation.

The Divisional Court in *R v Newcastle-under-Lyme JJ ex parte Hemmings* [1987] Crim.L.R. 416 cited *R v Best* (see this para. in main text) with approval when considering a committal charge of possession of cannabis *and* cannabis resin.

Cannabis Oil

9.03]   The question sometimes arises whether liquid containing cannabis comes into Class A or Class B. The position is clear under the Single Convention on Narcotic Drugs (see page 360 of the main work), where "cannabis and cannabis resin and extracts and tinctures of cannabis" are all included in Schedule I. However under the Act of 1971 "cannabinol, except where contained in cannabis or cannabis resin" and "cannabinol derivatives" are included in Class A, whereas "cannabis and cannabis resin" are included in Class B. Part IV of Schedule 2 defines:

> "'cannabinol derivatives' means the following substances, except where contained in cannabis or cannabis resin, namely tetrahydro derivatives of cannabinol and 3-alkyl homologues or cannabinol or of its tetrahydrol derivatives."

and "cannabis resin" is defined in section 37 as meaning "the separated resin, whether crude or purified, obtained from any plant of the genus cannabis". Applying these definitions is something of a puzzle.

Liquid cannabis is made by extracting tetrohydro cannabinol from plant material with a solvent such as alcohol. This is generally done by percolating the solvent through cannabis resin. The liquid is then allowed or encouraged to evaporate producing a more or less concentrated solution of the soluble constituents of cannabis or cannabis resin. Since resin is by definition an adhesive substance insoluble in water and cannabis is leaves and stalks, it would seem that what is dissolved is no longer contained in cannabis or cannabis resin. If therefore the analysis

22

finds that the liquid contains cannabinol or any of the substances listed in [9.03]
the definition in Part IV of Schedule the liquid is a Class A drug.
The opposite view is based on the decision in *Goodchild* (discussed in
this paragraph of the main work) and depends upon the view that by
dissolving or obtaining a suspension from cannabis or cannabis resin one
only changes the form of the substance but that its constituents are still
contained in naturally occurring material.

In the absence of any authority the authors can only put forward their
view that the process of dissolving the soluble constituents of a naturally
occurring material and concentrating them renders them no longer
"contained" in that original material. Therefore it seems, subject to the
results of analysis of individual consignments, that liquid cannabis should
normally come within Class A. If this view is wrong, then Schedule 2
requires amendment, because by concentrating the active ingredients the
maker is creating a more dangerous substance.

It was held in *Westminster City Council v Croyalgrange Ltd* [1986] [9.07]
Crim.L.R. 693 that if some evidence is raised suggesting that the defendant
held, or believed that he held, a licence then the court must be satisfied
beyond reasonable doubt that he did *not* hold such a licence.

The meaning of "supply" has been considered in two recent decisions. [10.03]
The facts in *R v Dempsey and Dempsey* [1986] Crim.L.R. 171 were that
a husband had been lawfully supplied with twenty-five ampoules of
Physeptone (methadone—Class A). (The irresponsible nature of the
prescription is not commented on in the report.) He asked his wife to
hold some of the ampoules whilst he went into a public lavatory to inject
himself. The husband was charged with supplying the drug to his wife
and she was charged with possession. The Court of Appeal allowed the
husband's appeal, holding that supplying the drug was not apt to
describe depositing it for safe-keeping. The wife's appeal was rejected.
She did not come within the terms of section 5(4)(b) of the 1971 Act nor
within Regulation 6(f) or 10(2) of the 1973 Regulations (Appendix IV of
the main work).

In *R v Magginis* [1986] Crim.L.R. 237; (1986) 82 Cr.App.R. 351 the
defendant was charged with possession with intent to supply. He pleaded
guilty (after securing a direction on the law from the judge) on the basis
that cannabis resin had been left in his car by a friend and he expected the
friend to come back and collect it. The Court of Appeal preferred the
decision in *Dempsey* to that in *Delgado* (*supra* in the main work) and
allowed the appeal. The Court held:

"We agree with the view of the Court in *Dempsey* that for there to be a
supply there must be a transfer of physical control which is for the benefit

23

[10.03]   of the recipient of the article. Mr. Forrester, for the Crown, accepted that this was the correct formulation but argued that the transferee obtains a benefit when he receives back an article which he has placed in the custody of another. The only discernible benefit is the resumption of actual possession. We do not accept that this is sufficient to constitute the return of an article as an act of supply."

The Court apparently substituted a conviction for possession simpliciter. The Court pointed out that having regard to the provisions of section 37(3) of the Act of 1971 the owner of the drug could be prosecuted for possession.

The decision of the Court of Appeal in *Magginis* was reversed by the House of Lords (1987) 85 Cr.App.R. 127. Lord Keith of Kinkel approved the Scottish case of *Donnelly v H.M. Advocate* 1985 S.L.T. 243 (para. 11.09 *infra*). In delivering the majority opinion he formulated the question for their Lordships as:

"Whether a person in unlawful possession of a controlled drug which has been deposited with him for safe keeping has the intent to supply that drug to another if his intention is to return the drug to the person who deposited it with him."

and answered in the affirmative. He distinguished *Delgado* (this para. of main work) from *Dempsey* (*supra*) on the grounds that Delgado intended to return the drugs to the persons who deposited them with him and thus put them into circulation, whereas Mr Dempsey merely gave the drugs to his wife for temporary custody—there was no intention that she should use the drugs for her own purposes. To consitute the offence the transfer must be for the purposes of the transferee.

A doctor giving a prescription for drugs does not "supply" them: *R v Taylor* [1986] Crim.L.R. 680 (Crown Court).

[10.05]   The case of *Blake and O'Connor* (1979) 68 Cr.App.R. 1 was concerned with section 4(3)(c) of the Act of 1971. The Court of Appeal had to consider the meaning of section 4(3)(b) in *R v Hughes* (1985) 81 Cr.App.R. 344. In its judgment the Court (Gore LJ) said:

"It appears to us that, for an offence to be shown to have been committed contrary to subection (b) or subsection (c) as the case may be, the prosecution has to prove (1) the supply of a drug to another, or, as the case may be, the making of an offer to supply a drug to another, in contravention of section 4(1) of the Act; (2) participation by the defendant in an enterprise involving such supply or, as the case may be, such offer to supply; and (3) knowledge by the defendant of the nature of the enterprise; i.e. that it involved supply of a drug or, as the case may be, offering to supply a drug."

The trial judge must explain to the jury the ingredients of the offence and assist them with regard to the meaning of "concerned in" and the

relevant evidence of the defendant's conduct in relation to that particular [10.05]
aspect of the case.

The position of an addict who injected a Class A drug (dextromoramide) [10.07]
into the arm of a visitor at his request came before the courts again
at the trial of *Gary John Austin* at St. Albans Crown Court, 20 February
1986 (unreported). Austin had been committed for trial as the result of a
private prosecution undertaken by Mrs. Williams, the mother of John
Williams, who died some hours after the injection.

The evidence of the defendant was that Williams himself prepared a
mixture of oral dextromoramide (Palfium) and tap water in a syringe
provided by the defendant. Williams had brought the tablet with him to
the defendant's flat. The defendant found a vein in Williams's arm and
placed the needle in it so that Williams could push the syrnge. Some of
the drug may have entered the blood whilst the defendant was carrying
out this operation. Williams rapidly developed symptoms of distress and
died from oedema of the lungs. Only traces of the drug were found in his
body at the post mortem examination.

The medical evidence was that pulmonary oedema is well known as a
cause of death following the intravenous injection of opioids. There are
dangers in intravenous injection of all drugs—not only of controlled
drugs. Fatalities from injections of opioids can arise from two principal
causes. Firstly, any opioid can depress breathing through direct action on
the respiratory centre of the brain. Secondly, such an injection may result
in pulmonary oedema—a massive outpouring of fluid into the lungs. The
exact pathology is obscure. The effect may be produced by small
quantities of the drug and also, perhaps, by contaminants. The size of the
dose is only one factor. The peak blood level occurs immediately after the
injection and thereafter falls very rapidly so that in four hours nearly all
the drug has disappeared (see table at para. 2.08A *supra*). Previous
experience of misuse of the same drug does not reduce the danger of
oedema. Austin was indicted for manslaughter and for an offence against
section 23 of the Offences against the Person Act 1861. Before
commencing his summing up to the jury on 20 February 1986 Mr. Justice
Staughton considered the judgments in *Newbury and Jones* (1976) 62
Cr.App.R. 291, *R v Cato (supra)* and *R v Marcus* (1981) 73 Crim.App.R.
49 (on the Offences against the Person Act).

On the count of manslaughter the jury were directed that there were
four ingredients: (1) deliberately (2) doing an unlawful act (3) which is
dangerous and (4) which is *a* cause of death. They were not concerned
with gross negligence or recklessness and the consent of the deceased was
no defence. On (2) the judge directed the jury that inserting the needle
was an unlawful act whether the defendant injected all or some or none of

25

[10.07] the contents. On (3) he directed that the act must be one that all sober and reasonable people would inevitably recognise must subject the other person to at least some risk of harm—even if not serious harm. On (4) he directed that the act does not have to be the sole cause so long as it makes more than a minimal contribution to death. It does not matter whether the defendant knew it was an unlawful or a dangerous act. The jury were asked to state what they found about the injection of the drug.

On the count under section 23 the jury were directed that there were again four ingredients: (1) maliciously (2) administered (3) a noxious thing (4) so as to endanger life. On (1) the judge directed that it was enough to find that the defendant deliberately inserted the syringe knowing at that time that it contained a noxious substance. On (2) "administer" could be taken to mean "inject" and it had to be proved the the defendant injected some of the drug into Williams. On (3) the substance injected must be a thing capable of causing injury to bodily health in the circumstances and quantities in which it was administered by the defendant. On (4) the judge directed that the jury would have to find that the quantity injected by the defendant did endanger Williams's life.

The jury found the defendant guilty on both counts on the basis that he had injected some of the drug in the syringe. The defendant, who had already served one year's imprsonment for a connected offence, was sentenced to fifteen months' imprisonment on each count, to be served concurrently.

The decision in *Dalby* was considered by the Court of Appeal in *R v Goodfellow* (1986) The Times 17 March; [1986] Crim.L.R. 468 when the court commented that what Lord Justice Walker had intended to say in the former case was that there must be no fresh intervening cause between the act and the death. The appellant had set fire to a house to obtain rehousing, with the result that the people inside the house died. The court set out the ingredients of manslaughter in almost exactly the same terms as Mr Justice Staughton used in *Austin*. The court followed *D.P.P. v Newbury* [1976] 2 All E.R. 365—a person who inadvertently causes death by an unlawful act which is also dangerous is guilty of manslaughter.

[10.09] **Attempt to Supply**

Anderton v Ryan and *Shivpuri* were considered in the appeal of *Tulloch* (1986) 85 Cr.App.R. 1. Tulloch was seen selling "tabs" which were supposed, erroneously, to contain lysergide. On arrest the appellant admitted that he believed that the tabs were impregnated with LSD. He pleaded guilty to attempting to supply a controlled drug on the basis that *Anderton v Ryan* had been correctly decided by the Court of Appeal. He appealed on the ground that the House of Lords' reversal of that decision [10.09] provided him with a complete defence in that it was impossible for him to have completed the full offence. The Court of Appeal concluded that the facts bore a close similarity to those in *Shivpuri*. Otton L.J. held that it was bound by its own decision in that case, which was at the time awaiting its hearing in the House of Lords, and dismissed the appeal. *Shivpuri* was subsequently upheld by the House of Lords—see 5.15 *ante*. (See also para. 10.08 of the main work.)

In *Crowe v MacPhail* 1987 S.L.T. 316 cannabis was found in an ashtray [11.03] appropriate to a prisoner's bed in his cell. He shared the cell with another prisoner and during part of the day other prisoners had access to the cell. When cautioned he said, "It wasn't exactly in my possession. It was under my ashtray. There is a difference." The High Court of Justiciary held there was sufficient evidence to justify the inference that he had control of the cannabis and that he had that control with the necessary knowledge.

The decision in *Buswell* (see para. 19.03 of the main work) was followed [11.04] by the Court of Appeal in the appeal of *R v Martindale* The Times 30 June 1986. In that case the appellant claimed that he had acquired a small quantity of cannabis in Canada two years earlier and had forgotten all about it. The Court of Appeal held that he remained in possession even though his memory of the drug had faded or gone. This decision ignores the fact that the appellant acquired the drug in Canada. If he at no time whilst in the United Kingdom knew that he had the drug in his possession, it is difficult to see how he committed any offence under the Act. It is also difficult to see how the decision in *Buswell* could be of assistance—that case decided that if a person had lawful possession of drugs prescribed for him, his possession did not become unlawful because he had forgotten about them; in other words, the exception under Regulation 10(2) of the Misuse of Drugs Regulations 1973 would continue to be available to him. That is very different from saying that the *mens rea* required on the date specified in the indictment can be carried forward from some earlier date. The decision also ignores the defence available under section 28(2).

The Court of Appeal has considered two cases concerning the concept of [11.04] possession.
    In *R v McNamara* (1988) The Times 16 February, the appellant had a box containing cannabis resin on the back of his motorcycle. He stated that he was doing deliveries for a man called "John" and thought that the

[11.04] box contained pornographic or pirate videos. The trial judge gave the following directions, which were approved by the Court of Appeal:

"You should convict the defendant if you are satisfied so as to be sure that he had possession of the contents of the cardboard box, which admittedly was cannabis resin, and knew that the box contained something, and unless on the balance of probabilities he had proved that he neither knew nor had reason to suspect that the box contained any controlled drug.

You should acquit the defendant, notwithstanding you are satisfied that he was in possession of the cannabis resin, if you conclude that he probably did not know, nor did he have reason to suspect, that the box contained a controlled drug."

The Court of Appeal summarised the speeches in *Warner* [1969] 2 A.C. 256 as follows:

"1. A man did not have possession of something which had been put into his pocket or house without his knowledge—'planted on him'.

2. A mere mistake as to the qaulity of a thing under the defendant's control was not enough to prevent him being in possession, for example, in possession of heroin believing it to be cannabis or asprin.

3. If the defendant believed that the drug was of a wholly different nature from that which it in fact was, then to use the words of Lord Pearce at p. 305 in *Warner*, 'the result would be otherwise'.

4. In the case of a container or box the defendant's possession of it led to a strong inference that he was in possession of the contents. But if the contents were quite different in kind from what he believed, he was not in possession of them.

The *prima facie* presumption was discharged if he proved or raised a real doubt in the matter, either (a) that he was a servant or bailee who had no right to open the box and no reason to suspect that its contents were illicit or were drugs, or (b) that, although he was the owner, he had no knowledge of (including a genuine mistake as to) its contents or of their illicit nature and that he received them innocently and also that he had no reasonable opportunity since receiving the package of acquainting himself with its actual contents."

The effect of section 2(3)(b)(i) of the Act of 1971 was that once the prosecution had proved that the defendant had control of the box, knew that he had control and knew that the box contained something, which was in fact the drug alleged, the burden was cast on him to bring himself within those provisions.

In *R v Lewis* (1988) The Times 16 February, the police raided a house of which the appellant was sole tenant. In the house were 42.5 grams of amphetamine sulphate and 1 milligram of cannabis. The appellant was not present. The defence case was that the appellant visited the house infrequently. Other people went to the house. In approving the trial judge's direction on the meaning of possession, the Court of Appeal held that what the authorities make clear is that the question is whether, on the facts, the defendant has been proved to have, or ought to have

28

imputed to him, the intention to possess, or the knowledge that he did [11.04] possess, what was in fact a prohibited substance.

Body Fluid

Consent to the taking of body fluid for use in evidence is not a [11.06] prerequisite of admissibility. The Court of Appeal so held in the case of *R v Apicella* (1985) The Times 5 December; (1986) Crim.L.R. 238; 82 Cr.App.R. 295, a case concerning rape. Lawton L.J. said:

"It was well established law that the way in which evidence had been obtained had no relevance to its admissibility, although its intended use in a trial by the prosecution might call for the exercise of judicial discretion to exclude it."

Section 78 of the Police and Criminal Evidence Act 1984 now deals with the taking of intimate samples where a person is suspected of being involved in a serious arrestable offence. Drug trafficking offences are made serious arrestable offences by section 36 of the Drug Traffficking Offences Act 1986.

Where a specimen of urine is obtained from a person suspected of possession of drugs or other offences not made "serious arrestable offences", admissibility would seem to be governed by section 78 alone.

R v Delgado would appear no longer to be the law—see 10.03 of this [11.08] supplement.

The High Court of Justiciary had to consider the sufficiency of evidence [11.09] in the case of *Donnelly v H.M. Advocate* 1985 S.L.T. 243, where the appellant had been found in possession of twenty envelopes containing heroin to a street value of £10 to £20 per envelope. It held:

"In our opinion where a large quantity of controlled drugs separately packaged in quantities normally sold in the streets, are found in the possession of a person, it is open to a jury to infer that that person intended to supply them to another".

(See also cases collected in new Chapter 14A *post*.)

The appeal against sentence of twelve years' imprisonment for conspiracy [11.10] to supply by *Salim Hafiz Patel* [1987] Crim.L.R. 839 turned upon the valuation of 1.99 kilograms of heroin with a purity of 55 per cent. At the trial a detective gave the street value as £750,000. On the hearing of the appeal the Assistant Director of Release gave a value of £160,000. Notice of this valuation had been given to the prosecution a month before the hearing. The Court then adjourned the case for the prosecution to call a

[11.10] senior officer from the National Drugs Intelligence Unit to attempt to resolve the issue. The Release valuation assumed that street level purity would be between 40 and 55 per cent. The detective had assumed a street level purity of between 7 and 9 per cent. Mr Galpin from the National Drugs Intelligence Unit had statistical information showing a mean purity of 40 per cent in recent samples from 85 seizures. The smaller the quantity seized, the more it had been "cut". He suggested an average street-level purity of 15 to 20 per cent. The Court of Appeal referred to the difficulties in arriving at a street-level value and warned:

". . . the use of the street value of heroin as a yardstick to translate quantities of the drug into financial terms as an aid to sentencing is to be regarded with caution. So long as it is relied upon as a rough yardstick we see no reason why judges should not measure the length of sentence to some degree by it."

The Court of Appeal made its own estimate as a figure of £300,000 and reduced the sentence to ten years' imprisonment.

For a detailed analysis of the difficulties posed by *Aramah* (para. 8.04 of main work) and the street-level value of drugs see the article by Les Kay in [1987] Crim.L.R. 814.

11.11   Conspiracy to Possess

In *R v El Ghazal* [1986] Crim.L.R. 52 the appellant arranged a meeting between T and C with a view to their making a deal about cocaine. When the three of them met, T and C arranged that C would purchase cocaine from a third party for T. The appellant went to the meeting with the vendor but left soon after as he knew that T and C were about to do "something funny" regarding payment. It was argued that the appellant's part in arranging the meeting was an act preparatory to the agreement and that it did not fall within the ambit of section 1 of the Criminal Law Act 1977. The Court of Appeal was referred to *R v Walker* [1962] Crim.L.R. 458—a case concerning an introduction with a view to the commission of robbery. In dismissing the appeal the Court said that *Walker* had turned on its own special facts and that the trial judge in the current case had correctly left it to the jury to convict if they were sure that T was asking to be introduced to C so that one of them could obtain cocaine and the appellant knew that was the purpose of the introduction. On those facts the appellant was entering into an agreement to procure cocaine for one of them. See also *Blake and O'Connor* discussed at 10.05.

Whilst it is a welcome development that it should be established that it is an offence to introduce one party to another with a view to one of them procuring drugs for the other, the theoretical basis of the decision is obscure, since the conspiracy does not come into existence until after the

introduction. Incitement to commit a conspiracy is not an offence   **11.11**
(Section 5(7) Criminal Law Act 1977)—perhaps the basis could have been
that the appellant counselled and procured the conspiracy.

Supply of Articles for Administering Drugs   **11.12**
The Misuse of Drugs Act 1971 was amended from 30 September 1986
by statutory instrument by the addition of a new section 9A contained in
the Drug Trafficking Offences Act 1986 section 34 and set out in
Appendix III to this supplement together with an amendment to
Schedule 4 providing for penalties.

The enacting of the section was inspired by the offering for sale of
collections of articles innocent in themselves but which when put together
added up to a kit for cocaine sniffing. No offence was committed because
the vital element, the cocaine, was missing. From 30 September 1986 it
is a summary offence to supply or offer to supply (but not to possess)
any article, other than a hypodermic syringe, which may be used or
adapted, either by itself or in combination with other articles, for the
unlawful administration of controlled drugs. It will also be an offence
under subsection (3) to supply or offer to supply any article which may be
used to prepare a controlled drug for unlawful administration. The
prosecution has to prove that the defendant believed that the article was
to be so used. This means that a shopkeeper will need to be very careful
when serving a known drug user—even an innocent pocket mirror or
razor blade has its uses in the administration of cocaine.

Subsection (4) in effect defines administration of a controlled drug as
being unlawful except in the circumstances outlined in Chapter 19 of the
main work. The maximum penalty is six months' imprisonment or a fine
at level 5. This provision applies in Scotland and Northern Ireland
(section 40(4)(b) and (5)).

The position in trials on indictment and in summary trials where section [14.04]
101 of the Magistrates' Courts Act 1980 applies is the same: *R v Hunt*
[1987] Crim.L.R. 263 H.L. (As to exceptions under Schedule 5 to the
Misuse of Drugs Regulations 1985, see para. 19.02 *post.*) See also
Westminster City Council v Croyalgrange (para. 9.07 *ante*).

For further cases on evidence see new Chapter 14A (pp. 44ff *post*).

See *R v El Ghazal* discussed at 11.11 of this supplement.   [15.01]

In *R v Panayi and Karte* [1987] Crim.L.R. 764 a yacht carrying cannabis [15.02]
to the Netherlands was intercepted in British territorial waters. The
appellants were convicted of assisting in the United Kingdom in the
commission of an offence punishable under a corresponding law in the

[15.02] Netherlands. The Court of Appeal had quashed the conviction on the grounds that no offence had in fact been committed in the Netherlands since the cannabis never got there. The prosecution were given leave to proceed on an alternative count of being knowingly concerned in the fraudulent evasion of the prohibition on importation. It is no defence that the route taken necessitated passing through British territorial waters—see also *R v Borro and Abdullah* (para. 5.09 of main work).

This decision may be contrasted with that in *R v Evans* (1977) 64 Cr.App.R. 237, where the appeal was dismissed. In that case the appellant had agreed whilst in England to fly to Brussels, pick up a suitcase containing drugs and deliver it in Canada. This he had accomplished. The Court held that the facts were indistinguishable from those in *Vickers* (see this para. of main work). It is not clear whether the convictions in *Vickers* and in *Evans* would have been sustained if the drugs had failed to arrive at their destination. In some countries there is no such offence as conspiracy so that there would be no corresponding law to be contravened before the drugs arrived.

[16.00] Most provisions of the Police and Criminal Evidence Act 1984 were brought into force on 1 January 1986 by the Police and Criminal Evidence Act 1984 (Commencement No. 3) Order 1985 (S.I. no. 1934).

Sections 56, 58 and 65 of PACE are amended in relation to drug trafficking offences by the Drug Trafficking Offences Act 1986 section 32. The amendments are set out in Appendix IX to this supplement.

Section 29(1) of the 1986 Act applies sections 21 and 22 of PACE to drug trafficking investigations as if they were investigations into offences. Section 29(1) is set out in Appendix IX to this supplement.

[16.03] Where police officers entered a café at night to search for controlled drugs
[16.04] without a warrant under section 23 1971 Act they were entitled to rely on their powers of entry under the Greater London Council (General Powers) Act 1968 and the Gaming Act 1945. The Divisional Court in *Foster v Attard* (1986) The Times 4 January; [1986] Crim.L.R. 627 held that once a police officer was lawfully on premises, no matter what power placed him in that position, he was lawfully there for all purposes. Lord Justice Watkins said:

> "Here the two Acts of Parliament gave the police officers the right to be upon the premises and accordingly, in searching the defendent they were in the execution of their duty if they had reasonable grounds for suspecting that he was in possession of drugs."

The Divisional Court accordingly allowed the appeal by the police against the dismissal of a charge of obstructing a police officer in the course of his duty.

It was contended that section 23 has been affected by section 18 of [16.03]
PACE to the extent that it only applies to searches undertaken before an [16.04]
arrest. Searches after arrest must comply with section 18. The Court of
Appeal without deciding the issue, expressed the view that this interpretation was wrong in *R v Mowatt* on 14 July 1987 (unreported). In that
case officers had followed the appellant in his car. When he stopped he
ran off. He was eventually captured. His car was taken to the police
station and, about an hour after his leaving the car, it was searched and
cannabis resin discovered. No authority was obtained from an officer of
the rank of inspector as is required for a search under section 18(4) of
PACE. The prosecution contended that the search was lawful under
section 23(2). The trial judge took the view that section 18 had been
breached and that section 78 of PACE therefore required the evidence to
be excluded but admitted it under section 23.

The Court of Appeal held that the search was authorised by section 32
of PACE. (The word "premises" is apt to describe a motor car: section
23 PACE). The escape and pursuit did not prevent him being described as
in the vehicle "immediately before he was arrested". In any case the
Court of Appeal did not see anything unfair in the breach of section 18
which would render it necessary to exclude the evidence of the search
under section 78 of PACE. A clear breach of a significant requirement of
PACE does not automatically require the exclusion of evidence so
obtained.

In *Carmichael v Brannan* 1986 S.L.T. 5 officers armed with a warrant to
search premises and any persons therein entered the premises. Three
persons jumped out of a window, one concealed himself and one
swallowed something. Lord Cameron held that obstruction does not
necessarily involve the use of physical force. The only limitation is that
the act must be intended to obstruct the police. He doubted if there was a
common law right to run away from the police. The following acts all
constituted obstruction:

(1) placing oneself in a position where a search of the person cannot be
achieved;

(2) simultaneously removing one's person so that one cannot be
searched;

(3) swallowing a substance so that it cannot be examined.

Serious Arrestable Offences [16.07]
Drug trafficking offences (including an offence of "laundering" under
section 24) are made serious arrestable offences by section 36 of the Drug
Trafficking Offences Act 1986. The relevant amendment is set out in

33

[16.07] Appendix IX to this supplement. Note that conspiracy, attempt or aiding and abetting a drug trafficking offence are not included.

The powers under the following provisions of the Police and Criminal Evidence Act can only be exercised in respect of serious arrestable offences:

Section(s)	Power
4	Road Checks
8	Issue of search warrants by justices
9	Orders or warrants issued by judges under Schedule 1
42	Authority to detain without charge up to 36 hours
43 and 44	Warrants of further detention
56	Delay in providing notification of arrest
58	Delay in allowing access to legal advice
62	Authority to take an intimate sample
63	Authority to take samples without consent

16.08 Body Fluid

In *R v Apicella* [1986] Crim.L.R. 238; (1986) 82 Crim.App.R 295 body fluid was taken from the appellant in the course of medical treatment. It was used in evidence at his trial for rape. He appealed on the ground that the sample should not have been taken without his consent. The Court of Appeal dismissed the appeal, holding that the admission of evidence as to what has been seen or found is not connected in any way with the rules relating to the admissibility of confessions. The case is discussed further at 11.06 *ante*.

16.09 Privilege of Informers etc.

The courts protect the identity of informers not only for their own safety but also to ensure that the supply of information does not dry up. This rule was considered in *R v Rankin* (1986) The Times 4 March; [1986] Crim.L.R. 464; [1986] 2 W.L.R. 1075, where the defence attempted to discover the exact location of an observation post from which the police had observed the defendant selling cannabis. The Court of Appeal held that the reasons which gave rise to the rule that an informer was not to be identified applied with equal force to the identification of the owner or occupier of premises used for surveillance and to the identification of those premises themselves. The rule is a rule of exclusion subject to a discretion to admit in order to avoid a miscarriage of justice. Even if the prosecution did not invoke the rule the judge was none the less obliged to apply it.

See also *R v Hallett and others* [1986] Crim.L.R. 462, a case concerning an importation of cocaine where disclosure was rightly refused.

See also *R v Ansari* [1986] Crim.L.R. 129: appellant supplied heroin to [17.03 small circle of friends; sentence of seven years reduced to five years.

The time has come to move up the level of sentencing for serious drug offences. The Court of Appeal so held in upholding a sentence of seven years' imprisonment for possessing cannabis resin with intent to supply in *R v Gilmore* (1986) The Times 21 May. The drugs involved were approximately 20 kg of cannabis resin and 20 kg of cannabis oil.

Manufacture of a drug is analogous to importing a drug of the same class. Sentences of 10 years' imprisonment (*R v Shaw* [1986] Crim.L.R. 485) and 7, 8 and 6 years on defendants according to their roles (*R v Morgan and others* [1986] Crim.L.R. 485) have been upheld in respect of conspiracies to manufacture amphetamine (a Class B drug).

Offences under sections 4, 5(3) and 20 1971 Act are specified in Part II of Schedule 1 to the Criminal Justice Act 1982. They are "excluded offences", so that offenders are not eligible for early release under section 32 of that Act.

The Home Secretary announced in 1983 that parole will be withheld from prisoners serving five years' imprisonment or longer for offences of drug trafficking. His power to adopt such a policy was upheld by the House of Lords in *re Findlay and others* [1986] Crim.L.R. 154; [1986] A.C. 318.

Trial within a Trial   [17.03

When the defendant pleads guilty on a basis different to that put forward by the prosecution there should be a trial within a trial to decide the factual basis of the sentence. In the case of *R v Cooper* (1985) The Times 5 December, the appellant pleaded guilty on the basis that he had only supplied drugs to his friends, whereas the prosecution contended that he had been seen in a public place supplying drugs for money. The trial judge passed sentence on the basis of the prosecution case. The Court of Appeal held that the trial judge should have followed *R v Newton* (1983) 77 Cr.App.R. 13 and substituted a lesser sentence which allowed of the appellant's immediate release.

In a jury trial the judge may obtain a verdict which reveals the basis of the jury's finding. Judges are usually reluctant to ask for a special verdict but it could be a sensible course in some circumstances. On a simple plea, the judge must accept the plea on the basis on which it is put forward by the defendant unless he hears evidence from both sides so that he can form his own conclusion. The question whether a trial of the issue should be held does not depend on the consent of counsel for the defendent. Unless the court is prepared to sentence on the basis of the plea it must proceed to a trial of the issue: *R v Smith* [1986] Crim.L.R. 640 citing *R v Williams and another* (1983) 5 Cr.App.R.(S) 134.

[17.03]   Where a defendant has pleaded guilty on a particular basis of fact, it is wrong for the judge to take account of differing evidence which he had heard in the course of a trial of a co-defendant who had pleaded not guilty: *R v Michaels and Skoblo* (1981) 3 Cr.App.R.(S) 188 approved in *R v Ghandi* (para. 8.04 *supra*).

Sentencing a defendant whose version of events or of his role in them differs from that of the prosecution has evidently exercised the Court of Appeal in recent months. If the defendant's version accepts the case for the prosecution but puts forward an account which mitigates the role of the defendant, the trial judge may make up his own mind without necessarily hearing evidence: *R v Bilinski,* [1987] Crim.L.R. 782 (see para.

[cont. p. 37

Some sentences which have been before the Court of Appeal

Drug and offence	Sentence	Reported
Amphetamine		
Conspiracy to produce	10 years	(1986) 8 Cr.App.R.(S) 16
Conspiracy to produce:		
principal offender	8 years	*Nicholas* C.A. 17/12/85
subordinates	$3\frac{1}{2}$ years	(unreported)
Small-scale dealers:		
one defendant	2 years	(1986) 8 Cr.App.R.(S) 94
another defendant	18 months	
Cannabis		
Cultivating 49 plants	1 year	(1987) 9 Cr.App.R.(S) 173
Conspiracy to supply	27 months	(1986) 8 Cr.App.R.(S) 217
Possess with intent (2.8 kg)	3 years ⎫	(1986) 8 Cr.App.R.(S) 384
small-scale supply	18 months ⎬	
Possession (50 g)	1 year Y.C.	C.A. 30/6/86 (unreported)
Cocaine		
Small-scale dealer (5.8 g)	4 years	(1987) 9 Cr.App.R.(S) 8
Heroin		
Small-scale dealers (one guilty, one not guilty plea)	5 years ea.	[1987] Crim.L.R. 212
LSD		
25,000 tablets (value £125,000)	7 years	*Carr* C.A. 4/8/87 (unreported)

See also para. 8.01 *ante*. For value see *Patel* [1987] Crim.L.R. 814 and para. 11.10 *ante*.

8.04 *ante*) and *R v Ogunti* [1987] Crim.L.R. 836. Where the version put
forward is in direct conflict with the case for the prosecution there must
be a trial of the issue: *R v Newton* (1983) 77 Cr.App.R. 13 and *R v Cooper*
(1985) The Times 5 December.

Mitigation

Instigation of an offence by police is relevant to mitigation if the offence
would otherwise not have been committed. Where it appears that the
offence would in any event have been committed when the opportunity
arose and the police provided an arranged opportunity there is no ground
for reducing the sentence. The Court must decide whether the police (or
an informer) acted improperly. If he stepped over the bounds of permissible behaviour in instigating the offence, that will lead to a substantial
reduction in sentence. These principles are established by the decisions in
R v Birtles [1969] 1 W.L.R. 1047 and *R v Underhill* (1979) 1 Cr.App.R.(S)
270. A recent decision on this subject is *R v Beaumont* [1987] Crim.L.R.
786.

Discounts for assistance to the police may be as much as half—see
para. 8.04 *ante*. If a defendant is to give evidence against his accomplice,
he should not generally be sentenced until after the verdict: see *R v
Ghandi* (para. 8.04 *ante*) and *R v Weekes* (1982) 74 Cr.App.R. 161.

Addicts

In *R v Yeo*, C.A. 27 June 1986 (unreported) the appellant's drink,
unbeknown to him, had been laced with LSD. This resulted in bizarre
and aggressive behaviour followed by charges of criminal damage,
assault causing actual bodily harm and wounding for which he was
sentenced to a total of two years' imprisonment. Between consuming the
drink and committing the offences, the appellant learned about the LSD.
The trial judge held that this knowledge made his subsequent behaviour
just as blameworthy as if he had taken the LSD voluntarily. It was
equivalent to a person driving after learning that his beer had been laced
with vodka. The Court of Appeal held that the situation was quite
different. The evidence suggested that he was not experienced in the effect
of drugs. Medical evidence showed that LSD produced unpredictable
results in behaviour. There was a residual element which warranted some
punishment and—taking into account that he was at the time suffering
from a recent bereavement—the total sentence was reduced to one of
three months. (The situation was complicated by sentences on other
counts.)

It is not a matter of mitigation that persons are forced to commit
crimes of dishonesty in order to raise funds to feed their addiction to

[7.03]   drugs. The Court of Appeal in *R v Hamley and Marshall* (31 July 1987, unreported) said:

> "Any person who voluntarily becomes addicted to drugs and commits crime to raise the necessary finance to feed that addiction, cannot rely on the fact of the addiction as mitigating the offences he commits. Indeed it would not be unreasonable to suggest that in some cases it would be a matter of aggravation rather than mitigation that anybody should commit crimes on that basis."

These words are doubtless salutory and anticipate countless mitigations which are bound to be put before the courts. It may be, however, that they are too harsh and betray a determination not to understand the nature of addiction. How many addicts would agree that they "voluntarily" became addicted? What is the position of the addict who has made every effort to come off drugs and has repeatedly failed?

17.04]   Where the appellant was stopped in a car with approximately five grammes of cocaine and there was evidence that it had at some stage been taped underneath a seat, forfeiture of the car under Section 43 of the Powers of Criminal Courts Act 1973 was upheld: *R v Boothe* [1987] Crim.L.R. 347.

17.05]   The fact that money seized by the police had been placed by them in a bank account pending a prosecution did not put it beyond the reach of a forfeiture order. The moment to be considered was the moment of seizure. The Court of Appeal so held in *R v Marland and Jones* [1986] 82 Cr.App.R. 134, a case concerning the profits of drug trafficking in Holland. The appellants pleaded guilty to two counts—conspiracy to contravene section 20 1971 Act and a specimen count of assisting in the unlawful supply of cannabis resin in a place outside the United Kingdom contrary to section 20 (the headnote of the report is inaccurate in stating that it was contrary to section 4(3)), and forfeiture was ordered of sums of money found where they lived, of sums in bank deposits and building society accounts and various items such as watches and cameras. Counsel at the trial conceded that the property related to count 2 and based their mitigation on the fact that substantial sums were to be forfeited. On appeal different counsel unsuccessfully argued that only a fraction of the property could relate to the actual count on the indictment. The Court held:

> "It would have been perfectly possible . . . to have included a large number of counts in the fresh indictment to cover this line of argument. It was not necessary to do so, because Counsel had made it abundantly clear . . . that they would make the concessions which they did."

It was conceded by the Crown that the money in the bank deposits and the building society accounts as choses in action could not be the subject

of a forfeiture order, nor could the produce of money such as the watches [17.05]
and cameras be forfeited as a result of "following the assets".
The Court of Appeal held in *R v Slater* [1986] 2 W.L.R. 988 that
section 43 of the Powers of Criminal Courts Act 1973 could only be used
to order the forfeiture of money used by the defendant himself for the
purposes of offences. It could not be forfeited on the grounds that it had
been used by other persons for the purpose of them committing offences.
The facts were that £1,136 had been found at the defendant's home and
the court was satisfied that this was likely to be the proceeds of selling
drugs. The defendant was convicted of conspiracy, so the money could
not be forfeited under section 27 of the Misuse of Drugs Act. It was
argued unsuccessfully that other persons not before the court who had
bought drugs had used the money to commit offences and that it should
be forfeited under section 43.

In *R v Maidstone Crown Court ex parte Gill* (1986) The Times 15 July
the Divisional Court was prepared to entertain an application for judicial
review of a forfeiture order made under section 27 of the Misuse of Drugs
Act where the property forfeited belonged to a third party. This was
because the third party, not being a defendant, had no right of appeal
against the order. The defendant had been convicted of supplying drugs
and two motor cars had been forfeited by order of the Crown Court. The
Divisional Court quashed the forfeiture order in the case of one of the
cars on the grounds that it had not been established that the words
"anything shown . . . to relate to the offence" in section 27(1) applied to
that car. The court went on to quash the order in relation to the other car
on the grounds that, although it had been used for the purpose of the
offence, the applicant, when he lent the car to his son (the defendant), had
no reason to suspect it was going to be used for an illegal purpose. The
court said

". . . there might be cases where a man who lent his car should have been
put on notice that the car was going to be used for some illegal purpose. In
these circumstances it might be proper for the judge to make a forfeiture
order."

Where a person makes representations under section 27(2) the court
has a discretion whether or not to order forfeiture. The Divisional Court
appears to be saying that the discretion should be exercised in favour of
an applicant owner unless he had some reason to suppose that the subject
was going to be used for an illegal purpose (but not necessarily that it was
going to be used in connection with a drugs offence).

R v Askew [1987] Crim.L.R. 584 and *R v Neville* [1987] Crim.L.R. 585
both concerned money found in the possession of suppliers. The Court of
Appeal followed *R v Morgan* (this para. in main work) and *R v Slater*

39

[17.05]   (ibid.) respectively and quashed the convictions. These problems should not occur in relation to any offence in which proceedings have been instituted since 12 January 1987, when section 1 of the Drug Trafficking Offences Act 1986 came into force (see Chapters 27ff *post*).

Drugs and criminal responsibility

17.07   Craving for drink (or drugs) such as to produce an abnormality of mind within the meaning of section 2(1) of the Homicide Act 1957 (i.e. diminished responsibility) would have to be such a craving as to render the accused's use of drink (or drugs) involuntary: *R v Tandy* (1987) The Times 23 December.

[18.00]   The Misuse of Drugs Regulations 1973 (S.I. No. 797) are revoked and replaced by the Misuse of Drugs Regulations 1985 (S.I. No. 2066) which are set out in Appendix IV to this supplement. The new regulations are a consolidating measure but they make some changes in the law. They came into effect on 1st April 1986.

The Misuse of Drugs (Safe Custody) Regulations 1973 (S.I. No. 798) are amended by the Misuse of Drugs (Safe Custody) (Amendment) Regulations 1985 (S.I. No. 2067) which are set out in Appendix V to this supplement. They came into effect on 1st April 1986.

Proclamations, orders and regulations can be proved by production of a copy printed by the Government printer or on the authority of Her Majesty's Stationery Office (Documentary Evidence Acts 1868 and 1882 and *R v Clarke* [1969] 2 Q.B. 91). Once proved it seems almost impossible to challenge the validity of regulations: *D.P.P. v Bugg* [1987] Crim.L.R. 625; but see *R v Reading Crown Court ex parte Hutchinson & Smith* [1987] Crim.L.R. 827.

[19.01]   Regulation 6 is now regulation 6 (general authority to supply and possess) of the 1985 Regulations. This regulation has been expanded to except from the provisions of section 4 (restriction of production and supply of controlled drugs) certain supplies including supplies for the purpose of destruction of the drug.

[19.02]   The 1985 Regulations contain five schedules of drugs:

The old Schedule 1 is now Schedule 5
The old Schedule 2 is still Schedule 2
The old Schedule 3 is still Schedule 3
The old Schedule 4 is now Schedule 1

Schedule 4 of the 1985 Regulations is a new provision applying to [19.02]
benzodiazepines, which have been added to Part III of Schedule 2 of the
Act of 1971 by the Misuse of Drugs Act 1971 (Modification) Order 1985.
The modification order is set out in Appendix XV of the main work in the
form in which it came into operation. Benzodiazepines are excepted from
most of the restrictions which apply to controlled drugs.

The new Regulation 5 is identical to the old one.

The new Regulation 7 is in effect the same as the old one except that it
refers to the schedules as re-numbered.

Regulations 8 and 9 are replaced by almost identical regulations with
the same numbers.

Regulation 11 is replaced by a new regulation 11 which is not limited to
authorising midwives to possess or administer pethidine. The authority is
now extended to include any controlled drug which she may lawfully
administer in accordance with the Medicines Act of 1968.

Schedule 5 relaxes controls over the preparations of drugs listed
therein. The relaxation is general—it has nothing to do with possession
by doctors or dentists as the Recorder erroneously supposed in the trial
of *R v Hunt* (1986) 82 Cr.App.R. 244. The Court of Appeal decided in
that case that it was for the accused person to establish that the drug
giving rise to a charge in fact consisted of a preparation listed in Schedule
1 (now Schedule 5). The House of Lords ([1987] Crim.L.R. 263) reversed
this decision on other grounds concerning the burden of proof when it is
claimed that a substance falls within an exception listed in Schedule 5.
Exceptions are provided for preparations which contain a very small
proportion of a controlled drug such as aspirin and codeine tablets, or
kaolin and morphine mixtures. Such preparations are sold in chemists'
shops in containers labelled to describe the drugs and their proportions.
Until 13 December 1986 it was generally thought that it was for the
defendant to bring himself within the protection of these exceptions. The
House of Lords has now held that the prosecution must prove that a
preparation, the subject of a prosecution, does not fall within Schedule 5.

Edwards (para. 6.02 of main work) established that the exception to the
fundamental rule that the prosecution must prove the elements of the
charge was limited to offences arising under enactments which prohibit
the doing of an act save in specified circumstances or by persons of
specified classes or with specified qualifications or with the licence or
permission of specified authorities. Where the offence is one of possessing
a prohibited substance the prosecution must prove that the form in which
the substance is possessed is a prohibited form. This means that where it
is permissible to possess a proportion of a controlled drug specified in
Schedule 5 and a preparation of that drug is the subject of a prosecution

41

[19.02]   the analyst must give evidence that the preparation does not come within any exception in that schedule. (See "Statutory Exceptions: A Third Knot in the Golden Thread" [1988] Crim.L.R. 31.)

[19.03]   Schedules 2 and 3 have kept their numbers and are largely unchanged except that the new Schedule 3 has been expanded.
Regulations 8 to 10 have kept their numbers but are modified insofar as they apply to drugs on ships and offshore installations.

[19.04]   Regulations 12 and 13 are unchanged.

[20.01]   Regulation 14 has kept its number.

[20.02]   Regulation 15 has kept its number (15(2)(b) contains the exception for phenobarbitone).

[20.03]   Regulation 16 has kept its number.
A doctor giving a prescription for drugs does not "supply" them—*R v Taylor* [1986] Crim.L.R. 680 (Crown Court).

[20.04]   Regulations 19 and 20 have kept their numbers but Regulation 22 is now 23.

[20.05]   Regulation 23 is now 24.

[20.06]   Regulation 24 is now 26.

[20.07]   The decision in *Storkwain* has been confirmed by the House of Lords (1986) The Times 20 June; [1986] 1 W.L.R. 903.

[21.00]   The Safe Custody Regulations have been amended with effect from the 1 April 1986 by the Misuse of Drugs (Safe Custody) (Amendment) Regulations 1985 (S.I. No. 2067). The Amendment Regulations are set out in Appendix V to this supplement.
The effect of the amendment is to exempt from the requirements of the Safe Custody Regulations such of the drugs listed in the Modification Order (set out in Appendix XV of the main work) as are specified in Schedules 3 and 4 of the Misuse of Drugs Regulations 1985 (set out in Appendix IV to this supplement).

[22.03]   Regulation 3(2)(b) makes it unnecessary for a doctor to furnish a notification if one has already been made within the last twelve months.

R v Best was approved by the Divisional Court in *R v Newcastle-under-* [26.04]
Lyme Justices ex parte Hemmings [1987] Crim.L.R. 416. An application
for judicial review was granted on the grounds that a committal charge of
possession of cannabis and cannabis resin was duplicitous. See *R v
Bellman* (1988) 86 Cr.App.R. 40 (para. 6.15 *ante*) on deception and
conspiracy.

The Court of Appeal has stated that an importation of heroin should be [26.05]
charged separately from an importation of cannabis because the maximum
sentences differ: *R v Van Thoor and Pijpenseel* (23 May 1986, unreported).
See also *R v Newcastle-under-Lyme Justices* (para. 26.04 *supra*).

Some Cases on Evidence

Evidence from telephone calls

14A.01 In order to prove that a person is supplying drugs from premises evidence is sometimes given of observations which establish an unusually large number of visitors over a period culminating with the arrest of one or more of them leaving the premises with drugs in their possession. In the case of *R v Harry* [1987] Crim.L.R. 325 the evidence available to the prosecution went one stage further. After the arrest of the appellant in P.'s flat an officer remained on the premises and recorded a large number of telephone calls where the caller asked for the co-accused P. and enquired whether there were drugs for sale. The appellant H. wished for the evidence of those conversations to be admitted to prove that P. was the dealer rather than him. The judge allowed in the evidence to the extent of allowing H.'s counsel to ask about the number of calls and whether any of them had been for H. H. appealed on the grounds that evidence of the contents of the calls was admissible to show the purpose for which P. was using his flat. The Court of Appeal held that the evidence was hearsay and therefore inadmissible. The cases seemed to show that if a servant or agent answered the telephone, this kind of call would be admissible to prove the purpose for which the premises were used (as in the case of brothels and massage parlours). However in this case the appellant wished to use the evidence to show who was using the premises—that it was P. and not H. This was a borderline case. Since H. wished to rely on the evidence "testimonially" it was hearsay. It was understandable that H. had a sense of grievance—however that was the law unless and until Parliament changed the hearsay rules.

14A.02 The fact of a telephone call is evidence, the contents are hearsay if they are put forward "testimonially" to establish the truth of any assertion made by the caller. This decision appears to say that the contents could have been put in to prove the nature of the business being operated, although they could not be put in to show who was operating it, which is relaxing the rule against hearsay. Words such as "Have you any cannabis for sale?" are only probative if they are understood as implying a statement that the caller has bought cannabis there before or has been told by a third party that cannabis is available.

14A.03 At the trial of Nigel Ratcliff and Helen Bland at St. Albans Crown Court evidence of phone calls received by the police after they had entered the defendants' premises was admitted. The callers were obviously seeking to obtain drugs and on each occasion they asked for "Nigel". No-one asked for "Helen". Miss Bland appealed ([1988] Crim.L.R. 41) but the Court of Appeal did not make any comment on the propriety or effect of admitting evidence of the telephone calls. The appeal turned on the sufficiency of evidence on two counts of possessing drugs with intent to supply. Observations had been kept and numbers of people had called at the defendants' premises and some of them were subsequently stopped and found in possession of drugs. When the police executed their search warrants both the accused were present, and drugs were found in a vacuum cleaner and traces of cannabis on a bread board and knife. The appellant denied all knowledge of the drugs. The prosecution case against the appellant was that she was living with Ratcliffe at a time when he was dealing in drugs. Reliance was also placed upon the traces on the bread board and knife. The Court of Appeal held that there was sufficient evidence from which the jury could infer knowledge on the part of the appellant that Ratcliffe was dealing in drugs but that there was no evidence that the appellant assisted or encouraged him in his enterprise. The trial judge should have ordered that there was no case to go to the jury.

Secondary evidence of exhibits

14A.04 As to admission of secondary evidence of exhibits which have been destroyed see *R v Uxbridge Justices ex parte Sofaer* (para. 6.14 *ante*).

Irrelevant evidence and the "true picture"

14A.05 In *R v de los Santos*, C.A. 3 July 1987 (unreported), after a raid on the appellant's premises she had pleaded guilty on one indictment to cultivating two cannabis plants and to possessing 1.96 grams of cannabis resin in a matchbox. She had pleaded not guilty on a second indictment to possessing amphetamine and to possessing quantities of resin with intent to supply it. The trial judge allowed the prosecution to prove the finding of the plants and matchbox and the appellant's pleas to the first indictment. (No reference appears to have been made to section 74 of PACE.)

The appellant contended that the evidence concerning the first indictment was irrelevant and attempted to rely on *D.P.P. v Boardman* [1975] A.C. 421. The Court of Appeal identified the issues as (i) the appellant's knowledge and (ii) her intent, and followed the decision in *R v Willis* (see

45

para. 6.14 in the main work). It was desirable that the jury should have before them a true picture of what was found in the house on that day and it was undesirable that the appellant should, if she chose not give evidence, be in a position to leave the jury to suppose that there was no cannabis in her house, or that she knew nothing about cannabis in general or about any cannabis in her house. See also para. 6.14 *ante*.

Police logs

14A.06 In *R v Sekhon* [1987] Crim.L.R. 693 a log was kept by a police inspector of observations by officers relayed to him by radio. The officers subsequently verified the entries. The inspector was cross-examined as to the contents of the log and it was eventually made an exhibit in the case. The Court of Appeal summarised the evidential effect of such a log as follows:

(1) It can be used to refresh witnesses' memory.

(2) It must be available for inspection by the defence.

(3) If cross-examination involves a suggestion of concoction, the record may be admitted as an exhibit to rebut the suggestion if the nature of the record assists on this issue.

(4) It may be admissible if it is inconsistent with the witnesses' evidence.

(5) In long and complicated observations it may be admitted as an *aide memoire* for the jury or to enable them to follow cross-examination on the contents of the log.

The status of the log will differ according to the purpose for which it is admitted. Normally it is not evidence of the truth of its contents. If it is admitted under heads (3) or (4), it becomes evidence by which the truthfullness of the witness can be determined.

CHAPTER 27

Introductory

Interpretation

27.01 The draftsman has relied throughout the Drug Trafficking Offences Act on definitions. These are found not only in section 38 but also scattered through the Act. Section 38(2) contains a list of expressions drawn from other provisions of the Act. In addition section 29(2) applies definitions from the Police and Criminal Evidence Act 1984 (PACE) for the purposes of sections 27 and 28, and section 10(7) applies definitions from the Charging Orders Act 1979 for the purposes of sections 9 and 10. "Drug trafficking" and "drug trafficking offence" are defined in section 38(1). The distinction between the two definitions is of profound significance. A person may be tried in a court in England and Wales for a drug trafficking offence and conviction sets in train the procedure for confiscating his assets. Institution of proceedings for such an offence or the fact that an information is going to be laid for such an offence is the prerequisite for making a restraint order or a charging order. The definition includes conspiracy, attempt and aiding and abetting a substantive offence.

"Drug trafficking" is more broadly drawn. It applies to activities carried out anywhere in the world. This means that section 2 (assessing the proceeds) applies to proceeds of trafficking outside the jurisdiction of the court. It also means that it is an offence under section 24 to "launder" proceeds of trafficking carried out anywhere in the world, and it allows the prosecution under section 27 (order to make material available) to apply to examine bank accounts or other material relating to persons suspected of trafficking abroad. Section 38(3) provides that the Act applies to property situated anywhere in the world. This means that a confiscation order can be made in respect of property outside the jurisdiction; if the defendant does not make arrangements for it to be brought within the jurisdiction for realisation, he will suffer an additional period of imprisonment under the default procedure applied and enhanced in its effect by section 6.

Other important definitions concern the institution of proceedings (section 38(11)) and the conclusion of proceedings (section 38(12)).

Commencement

27.02 Section 40(2) provides that the Act will be brought into force by statutory instrument and that the Home Secretary can appoint different days for the commencement of different provisions. High Court Rules and Crown Court Rules have been made governing the procedure under various sections of the Act. The whole Act was in force by 12 January 1987 (S.I. 1986/2145) so far as England and Wales are concerned. For Scotland the relevant provisions came into force on 1 January 1987 (S.I. 1986/2266).

Extent of Act

27.03 Unlike the Misuse of Drugs Act 1971, the Act applies only in England and Wales and not in Scotland, except for the provisions listed in section 40(4). By section 40(5) section 34 (supply of articles for administering drugs) applies in Northern Ireland—see para. 11.12 of this supplement.

CHAPTER 28
Confiscation Orders

(Readers may find the summary of procedure in the table on p. xxi helpful.)

Making the Order

28.01 Where a person is to be sentenced for the first time in the Crown Court for a particular drug trafficking offence, as defined in section 38(1), the court is required by section 1(1) to determine whether he has benefited from drug trafficking before sentencing him. Section 38(4) makes it clear that section 1(1) applies to offences committed before its commencement (12 January 1987) provided that proceedings have not been instituted by that day. Section 1 does not apply to committals for sentence of young offenders nor to appeals from a magistrate's court (sub-section (7)). Magistrates' Courts cannot make confiscation orders.

"Drug trafficking" is defined separately from "drug trafficking offence" and it is clear that the court must not confine its consideration to trafficking of which the defendant (or anybody else) has been found guilty. Section 1(3) has the effect that once a conviction has been recorded the court must take into consideration drug trafficking which took place before the commencement of the section. The defendant's whole career is to be examined to see if he has received any payment or other reward in connection with drug trafficking carried on by himself or by other persons, although the assumptions in section 2 only extend back six years. It does not matter if he has not benefited in respect of the offence for which he is being sentenced.

If the Crown Court determines that the defendant has benefited from drug trafficking, then it must determine the amount and order him to pay it. It must take account of the order before imposing a fine or ordering any payment or forfeiture, but it must leave the order out of account in determining the appropriate sentence (subsection (5)).

The court will not be restricted in its sentencing power by any legislation such as section 14(1) of the Powers of Criminal Courts Act 1973 (community service orders) only because it has made a confiscation order (subsection (6)).

Amount to be Recovered

28.02 The Crown Court has to assess the value of the defendant's proceeds of drug trafficking (section 4(1)). Nothing is said about deducting his costs and expenses. If the Court is satisfied that the amount that might be realised (see section 5(3)) from property available to the defendant is less than his proceeds, the amount to be recovered is the amount which it appears to the Court might be realised (section 4(3)). In other words, the defendant's liability is limited to the amount that he appears to be worth. In arriving at its determination the Court will have regard to the definitions in section 5 and to the provisions for tracing property and realising it. If property is held by the defendant or by a person to whom he has made a gift and it is outside the effective jurisdiction of the courts, the Act nevertheless applies to it (section 38(3)) and it will be included in the assessment as an asset. Section 4(2) provides that the Court may issue a certificate as to any matter relevant for determining the amount that might be realised and that it must do so if it is proposing to take all his property under subsection 3. This might be to the effect that the Court decided that the defendant's dwelling house was worth £X. If the house in fact sold for a lesser amount, the certificate would be relevant in proceedings before the High Court under section 14 for variation of the amount to be paid.

Statements by the Prosecution and the Defence

28.03 Section 3(1) makes provision for the prosecution to tender a statement as to any matters relevant to whether the defendant has benefited from his crime and by how much. The court may treat it as conclusive to the extent that it is accepted by the defendant. Such an acceptance cannot be used as evidence in a prosecution for an offence (Section 3(6)). The court can require a defendant to indicate to what extent he accepts allegations in such a statement and, insofar as he does not accept any such allegation, to indicate what matters he relies upon, presumably to refute such allegations (Section 3(2)). If he fails to comply with such a requirement, he may be treated as accepting every allegation except any allegation that he has benefited from drug trafficking or that any benefit was received in connection with drug trafficking—which reduces the effect of subsection (3) to such matters as ownership of property and date of acquisition. However if the defendant fails to contest a statement that he acquired, say, a house five years ago, section 2(3) will bite. Subsection 3(4) is the opposite side of the coin and makes provision for the prosecution to accept statements tendered by the defendant.

An acceptance or a challenge may either be in writing or given orally in court: on service see Crown Court (Amendment) Rules 1986 (Appendix XVII).

Assessing the Proceeds

28.04 Section 2 starts by defining "proceeds of drug trafficking" and provides that the value of the proceeds shall be the aggregate of the value or payments and other rewards. Section 38(5) makes this section apply to anything received partly in connection with drug trafficking and partly in some other connection. However section 5(5) allows the court to adjust its assessment of value to reflect subsequent changes in value of property and of money so that if, for example, a house was a reward or part of a reward, the value would be the current value of the house.

Subsections (2) and (3) are concerned with rebuttable assumptions which the Crown Court may make. They do not apply to the new offence of assisting another to retain benefits (section 24). These provisions reverse the burden of proof. The court may act on them unless the prosecution or defence shows that they are incorrect. It would seem that the burden of proof on the defendant is upon the balance of probabilities (see para. 14.02 of the main work).

The assumptions are limited in time to a period of six years ending with the date, as specified in section 38(11), when proceedings were instituted against him. This would apear to mean the proceedings leading up to the conviction for which he is to be sentenced. These assumptions are set out in section 2(3). They allow the court to assume that any property in the UK or overseas (see section 38(3)) held by the defendant since his conviction or transferred to him since the beginning of the period of six years preceding institution of proceedings was received by him as a payment or reward in connection with his drug trafficking (para. (a)). There is no gap. The period embraces six years before the commencement of proceedings plus the time that has elapsed between the commencement of proceedings and conviction. The court may also assume that any expenditure by the defendant during that period was met out of such payments (para. (b)). Thus the court can make assumptions from the fact that the defendant's way of life did not accord with his legitimate income. The court may assume, when valuing property, that the defendant received it free of any other interests in it.

Subsection (5) ensures that a recidivist does not have the same property taken into account in a second or subsequent confiscation order.

Enforcement as for a Fine

28.05 Confiscation orders are to be enforced as though the amount to be recovered was a fine but the periods of imprisonment in default are increased (section 6(1)). The court can allow time for payment or direct that payment be made by instalments. A term of imprisonment (or detention) to be served in default of payment will be consecutive to any period of custody imposed as the sentence for the offence (subsection (2)). Subsection (3) deals with concurrent sentences, suspended sentences,

51

youth custody or detention. A sentence in default will begin at the end of the substantive sentence—that is to say, the aggregate of sentences—but a suspended sentence is outside the ambit of subsection (2) as is the suspended part of a partially suspended sentence.

The section applies to orders made by the Court of Appeal and the House of Lords (subsection (6)).

The magistrates' court will not have power to enforce confiscation orders against young offenders' parents, nor will it have power to remit the whole or part of the amount to be recovered (subsection (4)) in respect of any defendant. No enquiry as to means will be called for.

If the defendant does not, in the event, have sufficient assets to meet the order, he is entitled to apply for variation under section 14. If he has assets but they are out of the reach of the court and of his receiver and he does not make them available, then he would be in danger that a warrant of commitment could be issued for default with the enhanced period of imprisonment. For appointment of a receiver see para. 30.01 *post*.

Definitions

28.06 Section 5 contains definitions of what property is or is not available to a defendant for the purposes of the Act (it is defined as "realisable property"). It does not matter that its acquisition had nothing to do with drug trafficking. In particular, property is available even if it has been transferred to another person since the beginning of a period of six years ending when proceedings were instituted for less than full value, or, where it has been received in connection with drug trafficking, if it has been transferred for less than full value at any time—"a gift caught by this Act" (subsections (9) and (10)); a gift made before section 1 came into force is included. Subsections (3) to (8) are concerned with arriving at the amount that may be realised at the time a confiscation order is made after making allowance for prior obligations.

Section 38(1) contains a number of definitions concerning property and the transfer of property, and in particular it makes it clear that the Act is concerned with real estate, choses in action and other intangible property as well as with money and goods. The restrictions which have been imposed on section 27 of the Act of 1971 will not apply to confiscation ordrs (see para. 17.04 of the main work).

CHAPTER 29

Interim Orders

When Interim Orders can be Made

29.01 The High Court may make restraint orders and charging orders when it is satisfied that there is reasonable cause to believe that the defendant has benefited from drug trafficking (section 7).

The power to make such orders is exercisable once proceedings have been instituted and before they have been concluded. These terms are defined in subsections (11) and (12) respectively of section 38. One event which can constitute the conclusion of proceedings is the satisfaction of a confiscation order.

Section 7(2) allows the court to exercise its powers to make such orders when it is satisfied that an information is about to be laid. However if proceedings are not instituted within a reasonable time, the High Court must discharge the order (subsection (4)).

Subsection (3) contains definitions which apply to sections 8, 9 and 22, when these powers are exercised before proceedings have been instituted. See R.S.C. Order 115 (Appendix XVIII).

Restraint Orders

29.02 Section 8 empowers the High Court to make a restraint order prohibiting any person from dealing with any realisable property (see definition in section 5). Dealing with property includes removing it from Great Britain (subsection (7)). The order may be made on an ex parte application to a judge in chambers by the prosecutor (defined in section 7(3)(b)). The order must provide for notice to be given to persons affected by the order. The order may specify conditions and exceptions which might, for example, provide for maintainance of the defendant's wife or children. The order may apply to property transferred to a specified person after the making of the order.

There is no provision for notice to be given of a proposed application nor for a person affected to have a right to be heard on the application. Advance notice would, of course, defeat the purpose of the order. However such a person (who might be the defendant) may apply in open court for a restraint order to be discharged or varied (subsection (5) and

53

R.S.C. Order 115, rule 5). The order must be discharged when proceedings for the offence are concluded.

Subsection (6) empowers the High Court to appoint a receiver to take possession of realisable property.

Subsection (8) empowers a constable, once a restraint order has been made, to seize property to prevent it being removed from the jurisdiction.

Charging Orders

29.03 Section 9 empowers the High Court to make a charging order in respect of certain interests in realisable property (see definition in section 7(3)). The purpose of the order is to secure the payment of any amount which may be recoverable under a confiscation order. If it is made in anticipation of a confiscation order it will extend to the full value of the property charged; if a confiscation order is already in existence the amount secured will not exceed the amount payable under that order. The order is made on an ex parte application to a judge in chambers by the prosecutor (see definition in section 7(3)(b)). There is no provision for giving notice of the application to affected parties nor for them to have a right to be heard on the application. Notice could, of course, have the effect of defeating the whole purpose of applying for the order. However persons holding an interest in property the subject of a charging order may apply for the order to be discharged or varied. Such a person could be the defendant. Rules of court are being prepared. The order must be discharged when the proceedings for the offence are concluded or the amount secured by the charge has been paid (subsection (7)).

Section 9(4) limits the interests which may be the subject of a charging order. These are interests held beneficially by the defendant or by a person to whom the defendant has directly or indirectly made a gift caught by this Act (see definition in section 5(9)) (a) in a list of assets set out in section 9(5) such as stock, unit trusts etc (the same list as in section 2 of the Charging Orders Act 1979) or (b) under any trust. Stock in a building society is excluded. Subparagraph (4)(b) deals with interests in property listed in section 9(5) held in trust and provides that a charging order will apply to the whole of the beneficial interest even though the defendant may be only one of several beneficiaries.

Section 10 contains supplementary provisions concerning the making and effect of charging orders and the application to them of existing legislation such as the Land Charges Act 1972.

CHAPTER 30

Realisation etc. of Assets

Appointment of Receiver

30.01 Where a confiscation order has been made and is not the subject of appeal the High Court may exercise its powers under section 11 provided that the proceedings have not been concluded. Proceedings are concluded, inter alia, when the order has been satisfied (section 38(12)). See Rules of the Supreme Court Order 115 (Appendix XVIII).

The powers under section 11 are to appoint a receiver (subsection (2)), to empower a receiver appointed under sections 8, 9 or 11 to take possession of realisable property (other than property subject to a charge under section (9)) and to enforce charges under section 9, to order persons to give possession of property to the receiver (subsection (4) and (6)) and to empower the receiver to realise it (subsection (5)). There is nothing to prevent the receiver realising legitimate possessions of a defendant in preference to realising the proceeds of drug trafficking.

The powers under subsection (3)(a) (enforcement of charges), subsection (5) (realisation of property) and subsection (6) (persons holding an interest in realisable property) shall not be exercised by the High Court unless a reasonable opportunity has been given to persons holding any interest in the property to make representations (subsection (8)). Such persons could include the defendant. The Act makes no specific provision for the giving of notice to such persons but a "reasonable opportunity" must imply some form of notification.

Subsection (7) ensures that the receiver does not duplicate the procedures under a charging order which are complete in themselves.

Application of Proceeds

30.02 Section 12 provides that sums recovered under section 8, 9 or 11 shall be applied towards the satisfaction of the confiscation order. Provision is made that the High Court may direct that payments should be made out of the property before it is used for satisfaction of the order—see however section 13(6).

Any surplus is to be distributed amongst those from whom the assets have been confiscated (which could include the defendant) according to directions from the High Court. Such people must be given an opportunity to make representations to the court before it gives any directions.

Exercise of Powers by High Court or Receiver

30.03   Section 13 directs that the High Court, the Court of Session and a receiver shall exercise their powers so as to ensure that the defendant's property is made available to satisfy a confiscation order. Where property has been transferred by the defendant for less than full value (section 5(10)) it is provided that the powers shall be exercised with a view to realising no more than the value of the gift (subsection (3)).The powers are to be exercised so as to allow persons other than the defendant or the recipients of such gifts to retain (or recover) the value of any property held (subsection (4)).

Subsection (6) makes it clear that the satisfaction of a confiscation order has priority over all other obligations. These would appear to include VAT, income tax arrears or alimony and "ordinary debts". However, obligations having priority at the time of making of the confiscation order will have been taken into account in calculating the amount that might be realised—see section 5(3).

Bankruptcy and Sequestration

30.04   Sections 15 and 16 deal with the effect on orders and property of bankruptcy (or sequestration in Scotland). Section 5(7) and (8) deal with the treatment of preferential debts under bankruptcy when calculating the sum to be recovered under a confiscation order and section 14(2) deals with the property of a bankrupt and sequestrated property on an application to vary a confiscation order. In general a bankruptcy will not affect powers that have already been exercised under the Act or property already subject to a restraint order, charging order or the proceeds of property realised by a receiver.

Scotland

30.05   Section 40(4) deals with the application of provisions of the Act to Scotland. In general the Act does not apply to Scotland, but sections 20–23 provide for the enforcement of orders made under the Act in Scotland.

Northern Ireland and External Orders

30.06   Sections 25 and 26 provide for the making of Orders in Council to allow the enforcement of confiscation orders or their equivalent which have been made in Northern Ireland or outside the United Kingdom. An order in relation to the USA was made in early 1988.

CHAPTER 31

Variation and Compensation

Variation of Confiscation Orders

31.01 Section 14 allows a defendant to apply to the High Court for a certificate that the property available is inadequate for full satisfaction of a confiscation order. If the High Court is so satisfied, then it shall issue such a certificate giving reasons. It must take into account the extent to which property held by a person adjudged bankrupt or whose estate has been sequestrated may eventually be distributed among creditors (subsection (2)(a)); but it may disregard any inadequacy in realisable property which appears to be attributable to anything done by the defendant for the purpose of preserving a gift caught by the Act (subsection (2)(b)). Bankruptcy and sequestration are dealt with in sections 15 and 16.

When a certificate has been issued the defendant may return with it to the Crown Court and apply for the amount in the confiscation order to be reduced with a consequent reduction in the period of imprisonment in default. However subsection (4) gives the Crown Court a discretion in the amount of the reduction. This is because it may have turned out that there are other assets which have realised more than expected when the order was made. There is no procedure for increasing the amount to be recovered under a compensation order if it turns out to be based on an undervaluation of assets. (R.S.C. Order 115(9), Appendix XVIII.)

Compensation

31.02 Section 19 provides for a defendant or another person holding property available in respect of the defendant to apply to the High Court for compensation in the event of an acquittal or of the case being dropped or a conviction quashed. Compensation can only be awarded where there has been some serious default on the part of the prosecution or of some person concerned in the investigation and the applicant has suffered substantial loss. The default must be such that if it had not occurred the proceedings would not have been instituted or continued. (R.S.C. Order 115(10), Appendix XVIII.)

57

Protection of Receivers

31.03 Section 18 protects a receiver who acts reasonably and believing that he is entitled to take action in relation to property which turns out not to be realisable property. It also provides for his payment by the prosecutor if insufficient funds are raised.

CHAPTER 32

Investigations into Drug Trafficking

General

32.01 Sections 27 and 28 provide new powers which are additional to those in the Bankers' Books Evidence Act 1879 and to the powers contained in Part II of the Police and Criminal Evidence Act. They extend to Scotland. The following definitions are incorporated from PACE by section 29(2):

"items subject to legal privilege"—section 10
"excluded material"—section 11
"premises"—section 23

These definitions will be found in Appendix IX of the main work.

Sections 27 and 28 provide for the prosecution to apply for an order or warrant to a Circuit Judge or, in Scotland, the sheriff, for the purpose of an investigation into drug trafficking. The application can be made as soon as the prosecution has reasonable grounds for suspecting that a specified person has carried on or has benefited from drug trafficking. There is no need for him to have been arrested or charged. Section 27(9)(c) states that an order may be made in relation to material in the possession of an authorised government department, defined in section 38(1) as an authorised department for the purposes of the Crown Proceedings Act 1947. A list of authorised government departments is published by the Treasury under section 17 of that Act. Section 28 is silent on the question of whether a warrant can be issued in respect of government premises.

Section 29 has the effect of applying PACE to material seized under sections 27 and 28. The expression "an offence" in sections 21 and 22 of PACE is expanded to cover "laundering" drug money (section 24) and sections 21 and 22 are made to apply to material produced in pursuance of an order under section 27(2)(a) as if it had been seized by a constable (which includes a customs officer—see definition of "constable" in section 38(1); although this effect is also achieved by Part I of Schedule 2 of the PACE Act 1984 (Application to Customs and Excise) Order 1985, set out in Appendix IX of this supplement).

Order to Make Material Available

32.02 Section 27 provides that a constable or the procurator fiscal in

Scotland may apply for an order to (a) take away or (b) have access to particular material, or, if the material cannot be specified, to material of a particular description.

Subsection (2), which is similar to paragraph 4 of schedule 1 to PACE, authorises the judge to make such an order if he is satisfied that the conditions set out in subsection (4) are fulfilled. The order will be directed to the person who appears to be in possession of the material unless it is in the possession of a government department, when any officer of the department who may for the time being be in possession may be required to produce it (section 30(11)).

All three conditions set out in subsection (4) must be satisfied. They are:

(a) that there are reasonable grounds for suspicion that a specified person has carried on or benefited from trafficking;

(b) that there are reasonable grounds for suspecting that the material is likely to be of substantial value to the investigation. The substantial value criterion is taken from paragraph 2(a)(iii) of Schedule 1 to PACE. A subsidiary part of this condition is that if there are reasonable grounds for suspecting that the material does not consist of or include items subject to legal privilege, or excluded material as defined in PACE, such items do not have to be produced (subsection (9)(a)).

(c) that there are reasonable grounds for believing that it is in the public interest to make the order having regard to the benefit likely to accrue. to the investigation and to the circumstances under which the holder is in possession of the material.

It will be interesting to see what interpretation the courts put on "substantial value to the investigation" as against "benefit likely to accrue to the investigation".

Subsection (5) empowers the judge when he makes an order for access to material to order any person to grant entry to premises for the purpose of access. A constable would have to apply for this supplemental order when different persons control access to the premises and to the material on the premises.

The Crown Court Rules 1982 (as amended) rule 25B cover discharge and variation of orders and proceedings relating to orders. An order has effect as if it were an order of the Crown Court, which means that failure to comply would be contempt of court. The maximum penalty for contempt of the Crown Court is committal to prison for two years (section 14, Contempt of Court Act 1981). Similar provisions apply in Scotland under the Act of Adjournal (Drug Trafficking) 1986 (S.I. no. 2184); see Appendix XVII in both cases.

Subsection (8) follows paragraph 5 of Schedule I to PACE and requires information stored on a computer to be produced in a visible or legible form. An order will override any obligation to secrecy or restrictions on disclosure imposed by statute or otherwise (subsection (9)(b)).

The Divisional Court had to consider the meaning of "items subject to legal privilege" in the case of *R v Central Criminal Court ex parte Francis & Francis (a firm)* (1987) The Times 7 December. The police were investigating suspected drug trafficking. They believed that the suspect used the proceeds to provide money for members of his family to buy properties. One such relative, Mrs G, was a client of Francis & Francis. The police applied under section 27 for the production of all files relating to Mrs G's financial transactions and dealings, and the application was granted. It was subsequently varied under subsection (6). The prosecution argued that the words "held with the intention of furthering a criminal purpose" (section 10(2) Police and Criminal Evidence Act 1984) were not restricted to a criminal purpose of Mrs G but extended to a criminal purpose of a third party. The defence argued that the only relevant intent was the intent of the party who was holding the papers, i.e. the solicitor, and relied upon the judgment of Glidewell L.J. to that effect in *R v Snaresbrook Crown Court ex parte D.P.P. and Akhoonjee* [1987] Crim.L.R. 824. The Divisional Court accepted that "the criminal purpose could be that of a third party as well as the client or if the client was an innocent beneficiary". The suspect's criminal purpose was sufficient to bring the case within subsection (2) and the prosecution was entitled to have access to the files. An appeal to the House of Lords is pending.

Authority for Search

32.03 Section 28 provides that a constable (which includes a customs officer: section 38(1)) or the procurator fiscal in Scotland may apply for a warrant in respect of specified premises. Subsection (2) authorises the judge to issue a warrant authorising a constable (or customs officer) to enter and search premises if he is satisfied that an order under section 27 has not been complied with *or* if the conditions in subsections (3) *or* (4) are fulfilled. The conditions in subsection (3) are:

(a) that there are reasonable grounds for suspicion that a specified person has carried on or benefited from trafficking; *and*

(b) that the conditions in section 27(4)(b) and (c) (see para 32.02) are fulfilled in relation to any material on the premises; *and*

(c) that it would not be appropriate to make an order under section 27 because:

(i) it is not practicable to communicate with any person entitled to produce the material, or

(ii) it is not practicable to communicate with any person entitled to grant access to the material or to the premises on which it is situated, *or*

(iii) the investigation might be seriously prejudiced unless immediate access can be obtained.

Subsection (4) provides for the situation where the material cannot be particularised. The conditions which must be fulfilled are:

(a) that there are reasonable grounds for suspicion that a specified person has carried on or benefited from trafficking; *and*

(b) that there are reasonable grounds for suspecting that there is on the premises material relating to the specified person *or* to drug trafficking which is likely to be of substantial value (whether by itself or together with other material) to the investigation but the material cannot be particularised; *and*

(c) (i) that it is not practicable to communicate with anyone entitled to grant entry, *or*

(ii) entry will not be granted without a warrant, *or*

(iii) that the investigation might be seriously prejudiced unless immediate access can be obtained.

Subsection (5) gives a constable (or customs officer) power, once inside the premises, to seize and retain any material which is likely to be of substantial value. He cannot seize items subject to legal privilege or excluded material as defined in PACE.

Information held by Government Departments

32.04 Section 30 provides that the prosecution may apply to the High Court for an order addressed to an authorised government department (see para 32.01 above) for the production of material to the Court. An order can only be made if the conditions set out in section 7(1) or (2) of the Act apply and (insofar as subsection (2) is relied on) a restraint or charging order is in force. The material in respect of which an order may be made is specified in subsection (3), but an order can only be made if it appears to the High Court that the material is likely to contain information relevant to exercising powers under sections 8 to 11—restraint orders, charging orders and realisation of assets (subsection (4)).

The section goes on to empower the High Court, once the material has been disclosed to the Court, to order its disclosure to a receiver (subsection (5)), and to order its further disclosure for the purpose of the functions of a receiver or the Crown Court subject to any conditions in the order (subsection (6)) and to the prosecution (subsection (7)), who may further disclose it for the purpose of their functions which would include prosecuting offences (subsection (9)). There are safeguards allowing an officer of the relevant government department to make representations before a disclosure order is made under subsections (5) and (7). These might be that the interests of an innocent third party would be revealed.

Subsection (10) makes it clear that orders override all statutory and other obligations to secrecy. There is no protection for items subject to legal privilege or excluded material if such should have come into the hands of the department. See R.S.C. Order 115(11) (Appendix XVIII.)

Inspection of Land Register

32.05 Section 33 requires the Chief Land Registrar to provide information relating to a specified person or property. Subsection (2) lists senior investigating and prosecuting officers who may make an application for such information and subsection (3) sets out conditions which they must certify are fulfilled. Subsection (4) provides for an application by a receiver, who must supply a certified copy of his appointment and certify that there are reasonable grounds for suspecting that the registrar has information likely to facilitate the exercise of his functions.

CHAPTER 33

Offences and Disclosure

Assisting Drug Traffickers

33.01 Section 24, which came into force on 30 September 1986, creates a new offence aimed at those who assist a trafficker by "laundering" or hiding his proceeds. It is a drug trafficking offence under the Act but section 2(2) (assumptions to be made) does not apply if it is the only offence for which a defendant is to be sentenced. It would also be an offence to assist a "launderer" to retain his profits arising from assisting a drug trafficker. For definitions of "proceeds of drug trafficking" see section 2(1) and of "drug trafficking" see section 38(1).

The offence is constituted by entering into or being otherwise concerned in an arrangement (see para. 10.05 *ante* for meaning of "concerned in") by which a person retains the use and benefit of the proceeds of his drug trafficking. Such a person is referred to throughout the section as "A". The *mens rea* of the offence is knowledge or suspicion that the person is a drug trafficker or has benefitted from drug trafficking. "Suspicion" must mean something less than belief, since the Court of Appeal has on many occasions, when dealing with offences of handling stolen goods, held that suspicion is not enough to establish knowledge or belief; see for example *R v Griffiths* (1975) 60 Cr.App.R. 14, discussed at para. 5.05 of the main work. The section would, for example, catch an accountant who advised a client how to transfer funds to a Swiss bank account, provided that the necessary knowledge or suspicion could be proved. Subsection (2) makes it clear that proceeds may be traced through various transactions and still be the subject of an offence.

It is a serious arrestable offence (see para. 16.07 *ante*).

Defences

33.02 Subsection (4) provides a number of defences which would need to be established by a defendant on the balance of probabilities (see paras 14.01 and 14.02 in the main work).

Those defences are:

(a) that he did not know or suspect that the arrangement related to any person's proceeds of drug trafficking. Since a defence only arises after the prosecution has established a *prima facie* case, the situation would be that the prosecution had proved that the defendant had, for example, been concerned in concealing A's proceeds and that he knew or suspected that A was a drug trafficker—following which the defendant could prove that he did not know that the proceeds were in fact the proceeds of drug trafficking. This he could do by proving either that he did not know that the property was connected with A at all or by proving that although he knew that A was a trafficker and that it was his property, he did not know or suspect that the property in question was the proceeds of A's trafficking;

(b) that he did not know or suspect that the arrangement helped A to conceal or retain the use of the property in question;

(c) that he intended to disclose his suspicions to a constable but he had a reasonable excuse for failing to do so. (This provision is concerned with subsection (3)—see 33.03 *post.*)

Protection for Disclosures

33.03   Subsection (3) is intended to protect, for example, bankers who reveal to the police their suspicions about funds in their hands. It is concerned with funds and investments which may be derived from or used in connection with drug trafficking. Such a disclosure is not to be treated as a breach of contract. Paragraph (3)(b) goes further and provides that acts done in contravention of subsection (1) shall not constitute an offence if they are done with the prior knowledge and consent of the police or disclosure is made as soon as possible afterwards.

Sentence

33.04   The maximum penalties are fourteen years' imprisonment and an unlimited fine after a trial on indictment, and six months or a fine not exceeding the statutory maximum (at present £2,000) on summary trial (subsection (5)). Early release will not be available (subsection (6)) under section 32 of the Criminal Justice Act 1982. For release on parole see para. 17.03 *ante.*

Prejudicing Investigations

33.05   It is an offence by virtue of section 31 to make any disclosure which is likely to prejudice an investigation. It is designed to catch those who might warn a suspect that his affairs are being investigated. The offence is only capable of being committed after an order has been made under section 27 or has been applied for and not refused, or a warrant had been issued under section 28. The *mens rea* is knowledge or suspicion that an investigation is taking place.

Subsection (2) provides two defences which would need to be established by a defendant on the balance of probabilities (see paras. 14.01 and 14.02 of the main work). These are (a) that he did not know or suspect that the disclosure was likely to prejudice the investigation, or (b) that he had lawful authority or reasonable excuse for making the disclosure. The second defence is designed to protect, for example, a person to whom an order is directed under section 27 but who is not able to comply with it without securing the assistance of another person who may have custody or possession of the material. If that third party warned the suspect, he might himself be guilty of an offence under the section.

The penalties are a maximum of five years' imprisonment and an unlimited fine on conviction on indictment, and six months or a fine not exceeding the statutory maximum (at present £2,000) on summary trial.

Misuse of Drugs Act 1971

Schedule 2, Misuse of Drugs Act 1971

Parts II and III have been amended with effect from 1 April 1986 by the Misuse of Drugs Act 1971 (Modification) Order 1985 (S.I. No.1995). The Order is set out in Appendix XV of the main work in the form in which it came into operation. In particular a large number of benzodiazepines are added to Part III but they are excepted from most of the restrictions which apply to controlled drugs by Schedule 4 to the Misuse of Drugs Regulations 1985 (set out in Appendix IV to this supplement) and by S.I. 1986/2230 (see below).

A new section 9A is added to the Act together with a consequential addition to Schedule 4 by section 34 of the Drug Trafficking Act 1986. See para. 11.12 of this supplement. Section 34 is in the following terms:

Drug administration kits etc

Prohibition of supply etc. of articles for administering or preparing controlled drugs.

34—(1) After section 9 of the Misuse of Drugs Act 1971 there is inserted the following section—

9A.—(1) A person who supplies or offers to supply any article which may be used or adapted to be used (whether by itself or in combination with another article or other articles) in the administration by any person of a controlled drug to himself or another, believing that the article (or the article as adapted) is to be so used in circumstances where the administration is unlawful, is guilty of an offence.

(2) It is not an offence under subsection (1) above to supply or offer to supply a hypodermic syringe, or any part of one.

(3) A person who supplies or offers to supply any article which may be used to prepare a controlled drug for administration by any person to himself or another believing that the article is to be so used in circumstances where the administration is unlawful is guilty of an offence.

(4) For the purposes of this section, any administration of a controlled drug is unlawful except—

(a) the administration by any person of a controlled drug to another in circumstances where the administration of the drug is not unlawful under section 4(1) of this Act, or

(b) the administration by any person of a controlled drug to himself in circumstances where having the controlled drug in his possession is not unlawful under section 5(1) of this Act.

(5) In this section, references to administration by any person of a controlled drug to himself include a reference to his administering it to himself with the assistance of another".

(2) In Schedule 4 to that Act, after the entry relating to section 9 there is inserted—

"Section 9A.   Prohibition of supply   Summary — — — 6 months or level 5
              etc. of articles for   on the standard
              administering   scale, or both."
              or preparing
              controlled drugs.

The Misuse of Drugs Act 1971 (Modification) Order 1986
(S.I. No. 2230)

Made - - - - -   *16th December 1986*
Coming into Operation   *1st April 1987*

1. This Order may be cited as the Misuse of Drugs Act 1971 (Modification) Order 1986 and shall come into operation on 1st April 1987.

2.—(1) Schedule 2 to the Misuse of Drugs Act 1971 (which, as amended,[1] specifies the drugs which are subject to control under that Act) shall be amended in accordance with the following provisions of this Article.

(2) In paragraph 1 of Part I of that Schedule:
(a) in sub-paragraph (a) there shall be inserted, after the words "Cannabinol derivatives" the word "Carfentanil" and after the word "Levorphanol" the word "Lofentanil"; and
(b) there shall be added at the end of the following sub-paragraphs:
"(d) any compound (not being a compound for the time being specified in sub-paragraph (a) above) structurally derived from fentanyl by modification in any of the following ways, that is to say,
  (i) by replacement of the phenyl portion of the phenethyl group by any heteromonocycle whether or not further substituted in the heterocycle;
  (ii) by substitution in the phenethyl group with alkyl, alkenyl, alkoxy, hydroxy, halogeno, haloalkyl, amino or nitro groups;
  (iii) by substitution in the piperidine ring with alkyl or alkenyl groups;
  (iv) by substitution in the aniline ring with alkyl, alkoxy, alkylene-dioxy, halogeno or haloalkyl groups;
  (v) by substitution at the 4-position of the piperidine ring with any alkoxycarbonyl or alkoxyalkyl or acyloxy group;
  (vi) by replacement of the N-propionyl group by another acyl group;
(e) any compound (not being a compound for the time being specified in sub-paragraph (a) above) structurally derived from pethidine by modification in any of the following ways, that is to say,
  (i) by replacement of the 1-methyl group by an acyl, alkyl whether or not unsaturated, benzyl or phenethyl group, whether or not further substituted;
  (ii) by substitution in the piperidine ring with alkyl or alkenyl groups or with a propano bridge, whether or not further substituted;

1 By S.I.s 1973/771, 1975/421, 1977/1243, 1979/299, 1983/765, 1984/859, 1985/1995.

      (iii) by substitution in the 4-phenyl ring with alkyl, alkoxy, aryloxy, halogeno or haloalkyl groups;

      (iv) by replacement of the 4-ethoxycarbonyl by any other alkoxycarbonyl or any alkoxyalkyl or acyloxy group;

      (v) by formation of an *N*-oxide or of a quaternary base.".

(3) In paragraph 1 of Part III of that Schedule:

  (a) after the word "Camazepam" there shall be inserted the words "Cathine" and "Cathinone";

  (b) after the words "Ethyl loflazepate" there shall be inserted the words "Fencamfamin", "Fenethylline" and "Fenproporex";

  (c) after the word "Medazepam" there shall be inserted the word "Mefenorex";

  (d) after the word "Prazepam" there shall be inserted the words "Propylhexedrine" and "Pyrovalerone"; and

  (e) after the word "Triazolam" there shall be inserted the word "*N*-Ethylamphetamine".

(4) In paragraph 2 of Part III of that Schedule, there shall be added at the end the words "not being phenylpropanolamine".

The Misuse of Drugs Regulations 1985

(S.I. No. 2066)

The Misuse of Drugs Regulations 1973 have been revoked and replaced by the Misuse of Drugs Regulations 1985. The new regulations came into operation on 1 April 1986.

The Misuse of Drugs Regulations 1985
(S.I. no. 2066)

Made - - - -	*19th December 1985*
Laid before Parliament	*15th January 1986*
Coming into Operation	*1st April 1986*

ARRANGEMENT OF REGULATIONS

SCHEDULES

SCHEDULE 1—Controlled drugs subject to the requirements of Regulations 14, 15, 16, 18, 19, 20, 23, 25 and 26.

SCHEDULE 2—Controlled drugs subject to the requirements of Regulations 14, 15, 16, 18, 19, 20, 21, 23, 25 and 26.

SCHEDULE 3—Controlled drugs subject to the requirements of Regulations 14, 15, 16, 18, 22, 23, 24, 25 and 26.

SCHEDULE 4—Controlled drugs excepted from the prohibition on importation, exportation and, when in the form of a medicinal product, possession and subject to the requirements of Regulations 22, 23, 25 and 26.

SCHEDULE 5—Controlled drugs excepted from the prohibition on importation, exportation and possession and subject to the requirements of Regulations 24 and 25.

SCHEDULE 6—Form of Register.

SCHEDULE 7—Regulations revoked.

Citation and commencement

1. These Regulations may be cited as the Misuse of Drugs Regulations 1985 and shall come into operation on 1st April 1986.

Interpretation

2.—(1) In these Regulations, unless the context otherwise requires, the expression:

"the Act" means the Misuse of Drugs Act 1971;[1]

"authorised as a member of a group" means authorised by virtue of being a member of a class as respects which the Secretary of State has granted an authority under and for the purposes of Regulations 8(3), 9(3) or 10(3) which is in force, and "his group authority", in relation to a person who is a member of such a class, means the authority so granted to that class;

"document" has the same meaning as in Part I of the Civil Evidence Act 1968;

"health prescription" means a prescription issued by a doctor or a dentist either under the National Health Service Act 1977, the National Health Service (Scotland) Act 1978, the Health and Personal Social Services (Northern Ireland) Order 1972 or the National Health Service (Isle of Man) Acts 1948 to 1979 (Acts of Tynwald) or upon a form issued by a local authority for use in connection with the health service of that authority;

"installation manager" and "offshore installation" have the same meanings as in the Mineral Workings (Offshore Installations) Act 1971[2];

"master" and "seamen" have the same meanings as in the Merchant Shipping Act 1894;

"medicinal product" has the same meaning as in the Medicines Act 1968;

---

1 Section 37(1) (interpretation) of the Act was amended by section 52 of the Criminal Law Act 1977.

2 Section 1 of the Act was substituted by section 24 of the Oil and Gas (Enterprise) Act 1982.

"the Merchant Shipping Acts" means the Merchant Shipping Acts 1894 to 1984;

"officer of customs and excise" means an officer within the meaning of the Customs and Excise Management Act 1979;

"prescription" means a prescription issued by a doctor for the medical treatment of a single individual, by a dentist for the dental treatment of a single individual or by a veterinary surgeon or veterinary practitioner for the purposes of animal treatment;

"register" means a bound book and does not include any form of loose leaf register or card index;

"registered pharmacy" has the same meaning as in the Medicines Act 1968;

"retail dealer" means a person lawfully conducting a retail pharmacy business or a pharmacist engaged in supplying drugs to the public at a health centre within the meaning of the Medicines Act 1968;

"sister or acting sister" includes any male nurse occupying a similar position;

"wholesale dealer" means a person who carries on the business of selling drugs to persons who buy to sell again.

(2) In these Regulations any reference to a Regulation or Schedule shall be construed as a reference to a Regulation contained in these Regulations or, as the case may be, to a Schedule thereto; and any reference in a Regulation or Schedule to a paragraph shall be construed as a reference to a paragraph of that Regulation or Schedule.

(3) Nothing in these Regulations shall be construed as derogating from any power or immunity of the Crown, its servants or agents.

Specification of controlled drugs for purposes of Regulations

3. Schedule 1 to 5 shall have effect for the purpose of specifying the controlled drugs to which certain provisions of these Regulations apply.

Exceptions for drugs in Schedules 4 and 5 and poppy-straw

4.—(1) Section 3(1) of the Act (which prohibits the importation and exportation of controlled drugs) shall not have effect in relation to the drugs specified in Schedules 4 and 5.

(2) Section 5(1) of the Act (which prohibits the possession of controlled drugs) shall not have effect in relation to:

(a) any drug specified in Schedule 4 which is contained in a medicinal product;

(b) the drugs specified in Schedule 5.

(3) Sections 4(1) (which prohibits the production and supply of controlled drugs) and 5(1) of the Act shall not have effect in relation to poppy-straw.

Licences to produce etc. controlled drugs

5. Where any person is authorised by a licence of the Secretary of State issued under this Regulation and for the time being in force to produce, supply, offer to supply or have in his possession any controlled drug, it shall not by virtue of section 4(1) or 5(1) of the Act be unlawful for that person to produce, supply, offer to supply or have in his possession that drug in accordance with the terms of the licence and in compliance with any conditions attached to the licence.

General authority to supply and possess

6.—(1) Notwithstanding the provisions of section 4(1)*(b)* of the Act, any person who is lawfully in possession of a controlled drug may supply that drug to the person from whom he obtained it.

(2) Notwithstanding the provisions of section 4(1)*(b)* of the Act, any person who has in his possession a drug specified in Schedule 2, 3, 4 or 5 which has been supplied by or on the prescription of a practitioner for the treatment of that person, or of a person whom he represents, may supply that drug to any doctor, dentist or pharmacist for the purpose of destruction.

(3) Notwithstanding the provisions of section 4(1)*(b)* of the Act, any person who is lawfully is possession of a drug specified in Schedule 2, 3, 4 or 5 which has been supplied by or on the prescription of a veterinary practitioner or veterinary surgeon for the treatment of animals may supply that drug to any veterinary practitioner, veterinary surgeon or pharmacist for the purpose of destruction.

(4) It shall not by virtue of section 4(1)*(b)* or 5(1) of the Act be unlawful for any person in respect of whom a licence has been granted and is in force under section 16(1) of the Wildlife and Countryside Act 1981 to supply, offer to supply or have in his possession any drug specified in Schedule 3 for the purpose for which that licence was granted.

(5) Notwithstanding the provisions of section 4(1)*(b)* of the Act, any of the persons specified in paragraph (7) may supply any controlled drug to any person who may lawfully have that drug in his possession.

(6) Notwithstanding the provisions of section 5(1) of the Act, any of the persons so specified may have any controlled drug in his possession.

(7) The persons referred to in paragraphs (5) and (6) are:

(a) a constable when acting in the course of his duty as such;

(b) a person engaged in the business of a carrier when acting in the course of that business;

(c) a person engaged in the business of the Post Office when acting in the course of that business;

(d) an officer of customs and excise when acting in the course of his duty as such;

(e) a person engaged in the work of any laboratory to which the drug has been sent for forensic examination when acting in the course of his duty as a person so engaged;

(f) a person engaged in conveying the drug to a person who may lawfully have that drug in his possession.

Administration of drugs in Schedules 2, 3, 4 and 5

7.—(1) Any person may administer to another any drug specified in Schedule 5.

(2) A doctor or dentist may administer to a patient any drug specified in Schedule 2, 3, or 4.

(3) Any person other than a doctor or dentist may administer to a patient, in accordance with the direction of a doctor or dentist, any drug specified in Schedule 2, 3 or 4.

Production and supply of drugs in Schedules 2 and 5

8.—(1) Notwithstanding the provisions of section 4(1)*(a)* of the Act:

(a) a practitioner of pharmacist, acting in his capacity as such, may manufacture or compound any drug specified in Schedule 2 or 5.

73

(b) a person lawfully conducting a retail pharmacy business and acting in his capacity as such may, at the registered pharmacy at which he carries on that business, manufacture or compound any drug specified in Schedule 2 or 5.

(2) Notwithstanding the provisions of section 4(1)*(b)* of the Act, any of the following persons, that is to say:

(a) a practitioner;

(b) a pharmacist;

(c) a person lawfully conducting a retail pharmacy business;

(d) the person in charge or acting person in charge of a hospital or nursing home which is wholly or mainly maintained by a public authority out of public funds or by a charity or by voluntary subscriptions;

(e) in the case of such a drug supplied to her by a person responsible for the dispensing and supply of medicines at the hospital or nursing home, the sister or acting sister for the time being in charge of a ward, theatre or other department in such a hospital or nursing home as aforesaid;

(f) a person who is in charge of a laboratory the recognised activities of which consist in, or include, the conduct of scientific education or research and which is attached to a university, university college or such a hospital as aforesaid or to any other institution approved for the purpose under this sub-paragraph by the Secretary of State;

(g) a public analyst appointed under section 76 of the Food Act 1984 or section 27 of the Food and Drugs (Scotland) Act 1956;

(h) a sampling officer within the meaning of the Food and Drugs (Scotland) Act 1956;

(i) a sampling officer within the meaning of Schedule 3 to the Medicines Act 1968;

(j) a person employed or engaged in connection with a scheme for testing the quality or amount of the drugs, preparations and appliances supplied under the National Health Service Act 1977 or the National Health Service (Scotland) Act 1978 and the Regulations made thereunder;

(k) a person authorised by the Pharmaceutical Society of Great Britain for the purposes of section 108 or 109 of the Medicines Act 1968,

may, when acting in his capacity as such, supply or offer to supply any drug specified in Schedule 2 or 5 to any person who may lawfully have that drug in his possession:

Provided that nothing in this paragraph authorises:

(i) the person in charge or acting person in charge of a hospital or nursing home, having a pharmacist responsible for the dispensing and supply of medicines, to supply or offer to supply any drug;

(ii) a sister or acting sister for the time being in charge of a ward, theatre or other department to supply any drug otherwise than for administration to a patient in that ward, theatre or department in accordance with the directions of a doctor or dentist.

(3) Notwithstanding the provisions of section 4(1)*(b)* of the Act, a person who is authorised as a member of a group may, under and in accordance with the terms of his group authority and in compliance with any conditions attached thereto, supply or offer to supply any drug specified in Schedule 2 or 5 to any person who may lawfully have that drug in his possession.

74

(4) Notwithstanding the provisions of section 4(1)(b) of the Act, a person who is authorised by a written authority issued by the Secretary of State under and for the purposes of this paragraph and for the time being in force may, at the premises specified in that authority and compliance with any conditions so specified, supply or offer to supply any drug specified in Schedule 5 to any person who may lawfully have that drug in his possession.

(5) Notwithstanding the provisions of section 4(1)(b) of the Act:

(a) the owner of a ship, or the master of a ship which does not carry a doctor among the seamen employed in it;

(b) the installation manager of an offshore installation,

may supply or offer to supply any drug specified in Schedule 2 or 5:

(i) for the purpose of compliance with any of the provisions specified in paragraph (6), to any person on that ship or installation;

(ii) to any person who may lawfully supply that drug to him;

(iii) to any constable for the purpose of the destruction of that drug.

(6) The provisions referred to in paragraph (5) are any provision of, or of any instrument which is in force under:

(a) the Merchant Shipping Acts;

(b) the Mineral Workings (Offshore Installations) Act 1971; or

(c) the Health and Safety at Work etc. Act 1974.

Production and supply of drugs in Schedules 3 and 4

9.—(1) Notwithstanding the provisions of section 4(1)(a) of the Act:

(a) a practitioner or pharmacist, acting in his capacity as such, may manufacture or compound any drug specified in Schedule 3 or 4;

(b) a person lawfully conducting a retail pharmacy business and acting in his capacity as such may, at the registered pharmacy at which he carries on that business, manufacture or compound any drug specified in Schedule 3 or 4;

(c) a person who is authorised by a written authority issued by the Secretary of State under and for the purposes of this sub-paragraph and for the time being in force may, at the premises specified in that authority and in compliance with any conditions so specified, produce any drug specified in Schedule 3 or 4.

(2) Notwithstanding the provisions of section 4(1)(b) of the Act, any of the following persons, that is to say:

(a) a practitioner;

(b) a pharmacist;

(c) a person lawfully conducting a retail pharmacy business;

(d) a person in charge of a laboratory the recognised activities of which consist in, or include, the conduct of scientific education or research;

(e) a public analyst appointed under section 76 of the Food Act 1984 or section 27 of the Food and Drugs (Scotland) Act 1956;

(f) a sampling officer within the meaning of the Food and Drugs (Scotland) Act 1956;

(g) a sampling officer within the meaning of Schedule 3 to the Medicines Act 1968;

(h) a person employed or engaged in connection with a scheme for testing the quality or amount of the drugs, preparations and appliances supplied under the National Health Service Act 1977 or the National Health Service (Scotland) Act 1978 and the Regulations made thereunder;

(i) a person authorised by the Pharmaceutical Society of Great Britain for the purposes of section 108 or 109 of the Medicines Act 1968,

may, when acting in his capacity as such, supply or offer to supply any drug specified in Schedule 3 or 4 to any person who may lawfully have that drug in his possession.

[(3) Notwithstanding the provisions of section 4(1)*(b)* of the Act:

(a) a person who is authorised as a member of a group, under and in accordance with the terms of his group authority and in compliance with any conditions attached thereto;

(b) the person in charge or acting person in charge of a hospital or nursing home;

(c) in the case of such a drug supplied to her by a person responsible for the dispensing and supply of medicines at that hospital or nursing home, the sister or acting sister for the time being in charge of a ward, theatre or other department in a hospital or nursing home,

may, when acting in his capacity as such, supply or offer to supply any drug specified in Schedule 3, or any drug specified in Schedule 4 which is contained in a medicinal product, to any person who may lawfully have that drug in his possession:

Provided that nothing in this paragraph authorises:

(i) the person in charge or ˌacting person in charge of a hospital or nursing home; having a pharmacist responsible for the dispensing and supply of medicines, to supply or offer to supply any drug;

(ii) a sister or acting sister for the time being in charge of a ward, threatre or other department to supply any drug otherwise than for administration to a patient in that ward, theatre or department in accordance with the directions of a doctor or dentist.]²ᴬ

(4) Notwithstanding the provisions of section 4(1)*(b)* of the Act:

(a) a person who is authorised by a written authority issued by the Secretary of State under and for the purposes of this sub-paragraph and for the time being in force may, at the premises specified in that authority and in compliance with any conditions so specified, supply or offer to supply any drug specified in Schedule 3 or 4 to any person who may lawfully have that drug in his possession;

(b) a person who is authorised under paragraph (1)*(c)* may supply or offer to supply any drug which he may, by virtue of being so authorised, lawfully produce to any person who may lawfully have that drug in his possession.

(5) Notwithstanding the provisions of section 4(1)*(b)* of the Act:

(a) the owner of a ship, or the master of a ship which does not carry a doctor among the seamen employed in it;

(b) the installation manager of an offshore installation,

2A   Amended by S.I. 1986/2330.

may supply or offer to supply any drug specified in Schedule 3, or any drug specified in Schedule 4 which is contained in a medicinal product:

    (i)   for the purpose of compliance with any of the provisions specified in Regulation 8(6), to any person on that ship or installation; or

    (ii)   to any person who may lawfully supply that drug to him.

(6) Notwithstanding the provisions of section 4(1)*(b)* of the Act, a person in charge of a laboratory may, when acting in his capacity as such, supply or offer to supply any drug specified in Schedule 3 which is required for use as a buffering agent in chemical analysis to any person who may lawfully have that drug in his possession.

Possession of drugs in Schedules 2, 3 and 4

10.—(1) Notwithstanding the provisions of section 5(1) of the Act:

(a)   a person specified in one of sub-paragraphs *(a)* to *(k)* of Regulation 8(2) may have in his possession any drug specified in Schedule 2;

(b)   a person specified in one of sub-paragraphs *(a)* to *(i)* of Regulation 9(2) may have in his possession any drug specified in Schedule 3 or 4;

(c)   a person specified in Regulation 9(3)*(b)* or *(c)* or Regulation 9(6) may have in his possession any drug specified in Schedule 3,

for the purpose of acting in his capacity as such a person:
Provided that nothing in this paragraph authorises:

    (i)   a person specified in sub-paragraph *(e)* of Regulation 8(2);

    (ii)   a person specified in sub-paragraph *(c)* of Regulation 9(3); or

    (iii)   a person specified in Regulation 9(6),

to have in his possession any drug other than such a drug as is mentioned in the paragraph or sub-paragraph in question specifying him.

(2) Notwithstanding the provisions of sections 5(1) of the Act, a person may have in his possession any drug specified in Schedule 2 or 3 for administration for medical, dental or veterinary purposes in accordance with the directions of a practitioner:
Provided that this paragraph shall not have effect in the case of a person to whom the drug has been supplied by or on the prescription of a doctor if:

(a)   that person was then being supplied with any controlled drug by or on the prescription of another doctor and failed to disclose that fact to the first mentioned doctor before the supply by him or on his prescription; or

(b)   that or any other person on his behalf made a declaration or statement, which was false in any particular, for the purpose of obtaining the supply or prescription.

(3) Notwithstanding the provisions of section 5(1) of the Act, a person who is authorised as a member of a group may, under and in accordance with the terms of his group authority and in compliance with any conditions attached thereto, have any drug specified in Schedule 2 or 3 in his possession.

(4) Notwithstanding the provisions of section 5(1) of the Act:

(a)　a person who is authorised by a written authority issued by the Secretary of State under and for the purposes of this sub-paragraph and for the time being in force may, at the premises specified in that authority and in compliance with any conditions so specified, have in his possession any drug specified in Schedule 3 or 4;

(b)　a person who is authorised under Regulation 9(1)*(c)* may have in his possession any drug which he may, by virtue of being so authorised, lawfully produce;

(c)　a person who is authorised under Regulation 9(4)*(a)* may have in his possession any drug which he may, by virtue of being so authorised, lawfully supply or offer to supply.

(5) Notwithstanding the provisions of section 5(1) of the Act:

(a)　any person may have in his possession any drug specified in Schedule 2 or 3 for the purpose of compliance with any of the provisions specified in Regulation 8(6);

(b)　the master of a foreign ship which is in a port in Great Britain may have in his possession any drug specified in Schedule 2 or 3 so far as necessary for the equipment of the ship.

(6) The foregoing provisions of this Regulation are without prejudice to the provisions of Regulation 4(2)*(a)*.

Exemption for midwives

11.—(1) Notwithstanding the provisions of sections 4(1)*(b)* and 5(1) of the Act, a registered midwife who has, in accordance with the provisions of rules made under section 15(1)*(b)* of the Act of 1979, notified to the local supervising authority her intention to practise may, subject to the provisions of this Regulation:

(a)　so far as necessary to her professional practice, have in her possession;

(b)　so far as necessary as aforesaid, administer; and

(c)　surrender to the appropriate medical officer such stocks in her possession as are no longer required by her of,

any controlled drug which she may, under and in accordance with the provisions of the Medicines Act 1968 and of any instrument which is in force thereunder, lawfully administer.

(2) Nothing in paragraph (1) authorises a midwife to have in her possession any drug which has been obtained otherwise than on a midwife's supply order signed by the appropriate medical officer.

(3) In this Regulation, the expression:

"the Act of 1979" means the Nurses, Midwives and Health Visitors Act 1979[3];

"appropriate medical officer" means:

(a)　a doctor who is for the time being authorised in writing for the purposes of this Regulation by the local supervising authority for the region or area in which the drug was, or is to be, obtained; or

(b)　for the purposes of paragraph (2), a person appointed under and in accordance with section 16 of the Act of 1979 by that authority to exercise

3　Section 16 of the Act was amended by paragraph 86 of Schedule 1 to the Health Services Act 1980.

supervision over registered midwives within their area, who is for the time being authorised as aforesaid;

"local supervising authority" has the meaning it is given by section 16(1) of the Act of 1979;

"midwife's supply order" means an order in writing specifying the name and occupation of the midwife obtaining the drug, the purpose for which it is required and the total quantity to be obtained.

Cultivation under licence of Cannabis plant

12. Where any person is authorised by a licence of the Secretary of State issued under this Regulation and for the time being in force to cultivate plants of the genus *Cannabis*, it shall not be virtue of section 6 of the Act be unlawful for that person to cultivate any such plant in accordance with the terms of the licence and in compliance with any conditions attached to the licence.

Approval of premises for cannabis smoking for research purposes

13. Section 8 of the Act (which makes it an offence for the occupier of premises to permit certain activities there) shall not have effect in relation to the smoking of cannabis or cannabis resin for the purposes of research on any premises for the time being approved for the purpose under this Regulation by the Secretary of State.

Documents to be obtained by supplier of controlled drugs

14.—(1) Where a person (hereafter in this paragraph referred to as "the supplier"), not being a practitioner, supplies a controlled drug otherwise than on a prescription, the supplier shall not deliver the drug to a person who:

(a) purports to be sent by or on behalf of the person to whom it is supplied (hereafter in this paragraph referred to as "the recipient"); and

(b) is not authorised by any provision of these Regulations other than the provisions of Regulations 6(6) and (7)(f) to have that drug in his possession

unless that person produces to the supplier a statement in writing signed by the recipient to the effect that he is empowered by the recipient to receive that drug on behalf of the recipient, and the supplier is reasonably satisfied that the document is a genuine document.

(2) Where a person (hereafter in this paragraph referred to as " the supplier") supplies a controlled drug, otherwise than on a prescription or by way of administration, to any of the persons specified in paragraph (4), the supplier shall not deliver the drug:

(a) until he has obtained a requisition in writing which:

    (i) is signed by the person to whom the drug is supplied (hereafter in this paragraph referred to as "the recipient");

    (ii) states the name, address and profession or occupation of the recipient;

    (iii) specifies the purpose for which the drug supplied is required and the total quantity to be supplied; and

    (iv) where appropriate, satisfies the requirements of paragraph (5);

(b) unless he is reasonably satisfied that the signature is that of the person purporting to have signed the requisition and that that person is engaged in the profession or occupation specified in the requisition.

Provided that where the recipient is a practitioner and he represents that he urgently requires a controlled drug for the purpose of his profession, the supplier may, if he is reasonably satisfied that the recipient so requires the drug and is, by reason of some emergency, unable before delivery to furnish to the supplier a requisition in writing duly signed, deliver the drug to the recipient on an undertaking by the recipient to furnish such a requisition within the twenty-four hours next following.

(3) A person who has given such an undertaking as aforesaid shall deliver to the person by whom the controlled drug was supplied a signed requisition in accordance with the undertaking.

(4) The persons referred to in paragraph (2) are:

(a) a practitioner;
(b) the person in charge or acting person in charge of a hospital or nursing home;
(c) a person who is in charge of a laboratory;
(d) the owner of a ship, or the master of a ship which does not carry a doctor among the seamen employed in it;
(e) the master of a foreign ship in a port in Great Britain;
(f) the installation manager of an offshore installation.

(5) A requisition furnished for the purposes of paragraph (2) shall:

(a) where furnished by the person in charge or acting person in charge of a hospital or nursing home, be signed by a doctor or dentist employed or engaged in that hospital or nursing home;
(b) where furnished by the master of a foreign ship, contain a statement, signed by the proper officer of the port health authority, or, in Scotland, the medical officer designated under section 14 of the National Health Service (Scotland) Act 1978 by the Health Board, within whose jurisdiction the ship is, that the quantity of the drug to be supplied is the quantity necessary for the equipment of the ship.

(6) Where the person responsible for the dispensing and supply of medicines at any hospital or nursing home supplies a controlled drug to the sister or acting sister for the time being in charge of any ward, theatre or other department in that hospital or nursing home (hereafter in this paragraph referred to as "the recipient") he shall:

(a) obtain a requisition in writing, signed by the recipient, which specifies the total quantity of the drug to be supplied; and
(b) mark the requisition in such manner as to show that it has been complied with,

and any requisition obtained for the purposes of this paragraph shall be retained in the dispensary at which the drug was supplied and a copy of the requisition or a note of it shall be retained or kept by the recipient.

(7) Nothing in this Regulation shall have effect in relation to the drugs specified in Schedules 4 and 5 or poppy-straw.

Form of prescriptions

15.—(1) Subject to the provisions of this Regulation, a person shall not issue a prescription containing a controlled drug other than a drug specified in Schedule 4 or 5 unless the prescription complies with the following requirements, that is to say, it shall:

(a) be in ink or otherwise so as to be indelible and be signed by the person issuing it with his usual signature and dated by him;

(b) insofar as it specifies the information required by sub-paragraphs (e) and (f) below to be specified, be written by the person issuing it in his own handwriting;

(c) except in the case of a health prescription, specify the address of the person issuing it;

(d) have written thereon, if issued by a dentist, the words "for dental treatment only" and, if issued by a veterinary surgeon or a veterinary practitioner, a declaration that the controlled drug is prescribed for an animal or herd under his care;

(e) specify the name and address of the person for whose treatment it is issued or, if it is issued by a veterinary surgeon or veterinary practitioner, of the person to whom the controlled drug prescribed is to be delivered;

(f) specify the dose to be taken and:

    (i) in the case of prescription containing a controlled drug which is a preparation, the form and, where appropriate, the strength of the preparation, and either the total quantity (in both words and figures) of the preparation or the number (in both words and figures) or dosage units, as appropriate, to be supplied;

    (ii) in any other case, the total quantity (in both words and figures) of the controlled drug to be supplied;

(g) in the case of prescription for a total quantity intended to be supplied by instalments, contain a direction specifying the amount of the instalments of the total amount which may be supplied and the intervals to be observed when supplying.

(2) Paragraph (1)(b) shall not have effect in relation to:

(a) a prescription issued by a person approved (whether personally or as a member of a class) for the purposes of this paragraph by the Secretary of State; or

(b) a prescription containing no controlled drug other than:

    (i) phenobarbitone;

    (ii) phenobarbitone sodium; or

    (iii) a preparation containing a drug specified in paragraph (i) or (ii) above.

(3) In the case of a prescription issued for the treatment of a patient in a hospital or nursing home, it shall be sufficient compliance with paragraph (1)(e) if the prescription is written on the patient's bed card or case sheet.

Provisions as to supply on prescription

16.—(1) A person shall not supply a controlled drug other than a drug specified in Schedule 4 or 5 on a prescription:

(a) unless the prescription complies with the provisions of Regulation 15;

81

(b) unless the address specified in the prescription as the address of the person issuing it is an address within the United Kingdom;

(c) unless he either is acquainted with the signature of the person by whom it purports to be issued and has no reason to suppose that it is not genuine, or has taken reasonably sufficient steps to satisfy himself that it is genuine;

(d) before the date specified in the prescription;

(e) subject to paragraph (3), later than thirteen weeks after the date specified in the prescription.

(2) Subject to paragraph (3), a person supplying on prescription a controlled drug other than a drug specified in Schedule 4 or 5 shall, at the time of the supply, mark on the prescription the date on which the drug is supplied and, unless it is a health prescription, shall retain the prescription on the premises from which the drug was supplied.

(3) In the case of a prescription containing a controlled drug other than a drug specified in Schedule 4 or 5, which contains a direction that specified instalments of the total amount may be supplied at stated intervals, the person supplying the drug shall not do so otherwise than in accordance with that direction and:

(a) paragraph (1) shall have effect as if for the requirement contained in sub-paragraph (e) thereof there were substituted a requirement that the occasion on which the first instalment is supplied shall not be later than thirteen weeks after the date specified in the prescription;

(b) paragraph (2) shall have effect as if for the words "at the time of the supply" there were substituted the words "on each occasion on which an instalment is supplied".

Exemption for certain prescriptions

17. Nothing in Regulations 15 and 16 shall have effect in relation to a prescription issued for the purposes of a scheme for testing the quality or amount of the drugs, preparations and appliances supplied under the National Health Service Act 1977 or the National Health Service (Scotland) Act 1978 and the Regulations made thereunder or to any prescriptions issued for the purposes of the Food and Drugs (Scotland) Act 1956 to a sampling officer within the meaning of that Act or for the purposes of the Medicines Act 1968 to a sampling officer within the meaning of that Act.

Marking of bottles and other containers

18.—(1) Subject to paragraph (2), no person shall supply a controlled drug otherwise than in a bottle, package or other container which is plainly marked:

(a) in the case of a controlled drug other than a preparation, with the amount of the drug contained therein;

(b) in the case of a controlled drug which is a preparation:
(i) made up into tablets, capsules or other dosage units, with the amount of each component (being a controlled drug) of the preparation in each dosage unit and the number of dosage units in the bottle, package or other container;

(ii) not made up as aforesaid, with the total amount of the preparation in the bottle, package or other container and the percentage of each of its components which is a controlled drug.

(2) Nothing in this Regulation shall have effect in relation to:

(a) the drugs specified in Schedules 4 and 5 or poppy-straw;
(b) the supply of a controlled drug by or on the prescription of a practitioner;
(c) the supply of a controlled drug for administration in a clinical trial or a medicinal test on animals.

(3) In this Regulation, the expressions "clinical trial" and "medicinal test on animals" have the same meaning as in the Medicines Act 1968.

Record-keeping requirements in respect of drugs in Schedule 1 and 2

19.—(1) Subject to paragraph (3) and Regulation 21, every person authorised by or under Regulation 5 or 8 to supply any drug specified in Schedule 1 or 2 shall comply with the following requirements, that is to say:

(a) he shall, in accordance with the provisions of this Regulation and of Regulation 20, keep a register and shall enter therein in chronological sequence in the form specified in Part I or Part II of Schedule 6, as the case may require, particulars of every quantity of a drug specified in Schedule 1 or 2 obtained by him and of every quantity of such a drug supplied (whether by way of administration or otherwise) by him whether to persons within or outside Great Britain;
(b) he shall use a separate register or separate part of the register for entries made in respect of each class of drugs, and each of the drugs specified in paragraphs 1 and 3 of Schedule 1 and paragraphs 1, 3 and 6 of Schedule 2 together with its salts and any preparation or other product containing it or any of its salts shall be treated as a separate class, so however that any stereoisomeric form of a drug or its salts shall be classed with that drug.

(2) Nothing in paragraph (1) shall be taken as preventing the use of a separate section within a register or separate part of a register in respect of different drugs or strengths of drugs comprised within the class of drugs to which that register or separate part relates.

(3) The foregoing provisions of this Regulation shall not have effect in relation to:

(a) in the case of a drug supplied to him for the purpose of destruction in pursuance of Regulation 6(2) or (3), a practitioner or pharmacist;
(b) a person licensed under Regulation 5 to supply any drug, where the licence so directs; or
(c) the sister or acting sister for the time being in charge of a ward, theatre or other department in a hospital or nursing home.

Requirements as to registers

20. Any person required to keep a register under Regulation 19 shall comply with the following requirements, that is to say:

(a) the class of drugs to which the entries on any page of any such register relate shall be specified at the head of that page;

(b) every entry required to be made under Regulation 19 in such a register shall be made on the day on which the drug is obtained or, as the case may be, on which the transaction in respect of the supply of the drug by the person required to make the entry takes place or, if that is not reasonably practicable, on the day next following that day;

(c) no cancellation, obliteration or alteration of any such entry shall be made, and a correction of such an entry shall be made only by way of marginal note or footnote which shall specify the date on which the correction is made;

(d) every such entry and every correction of such an entry shall be made in ink or otherwise so as to be indelible;

(e) such a register shall not be used for any purpose other than the purposes of these Regulations;

(f) a separate register shall be kept in respect of each premises at which the person required to keep the register carries on his business or occupation, but subject to that not more than one register shall be kept at one time in respect of each class of drugs in respect of which he is required to keep a separate register, so, however, that a separate register may, with the approval of the Secretary of State, be kept in respect of each department of the business carried on by him;

(g) every such register in which entries are currently being made shall be kept at the premises to which it relates.

Record-keeping requirements in respect of drugs in Schedule 2 in particular cases

21.—(1) Where a drug specified in Schedule 2 is supplied in accordance with Regulation 8(5)(a)(i) to any person on a ship, an entry in the official log book required to be kept under the Merchant Shipping Acts or, in the case of a ship which is not required to carry such an official logbook, a report signed by the master of the ship, shall, notwithstanding anything in these Regulations, be a sufficient record of the supply if the entry or report specifies the drug supplied and, in the case of a report, it is delivered as soon as may be to a superintendent at a Marine Office established and maintained under the Merchant Shipping Acts.

(2) Where a drug specified in Schedule 2 is supplied in accordance with Regulation 8(5)(b)(i) to a person on an offshore installation, an entry in the installation logbook required to be maintained under the Offshore Installations (Logbooks and Registration of Death) Regulations 1972[4] which specifies the drug supplied shall, notwithstanding anything in these Regulations, be a sufficient record of the supply.

(3) A midwife authorised by Regulation 11(1) to have any drug specified in Schedule 2 in her possession shall:

(a) on each occasion on which she obtains a supply of such a drug, enter in a book kept by her and used solely for the purposes of this paragraph the date, the name and address of the person from whom the drug was obtained, the amount obtained and the form in which it was obtained; and

(b) on administering such a drug to a patient, enter in the said book as soon as practicable the name and address of the patient, the amount administered and the form in which it was administered.

4 S.I. 1972/1542.

Record-keeping requirements in respect of drugs in Schedule 3 and 4

22.—(1) Every person who is authorised under Regulation 5 or 9(1)*(c)* to produce any drug specified in Schedule 3 or 4 shall make a record of each quantity of such a drug produced by him.

(2) Every person who is authorised by or under any provision of the Act to import or export any drug specified in Schedule 3 shall make a record of each quantity of such a drug imported or exported by him.

(3) Every person who is authorised under Regulation 9(4) to supply any drug specified in Schedule 4 shall make a record of each quantity of such a drug imported or exported by him.

(4) Paragraph (2) shall not have effect in relation to a person licensed under the Act to import or export any drug where the licence so directs.

Preservation of registers, books and other documents

23.—(1) All registers and books kept in pursuance or Regulation 19 or 21(3) shall be preserved for a period of two years from the date on which the last entry therein is made.

(2) Every record made in pursuance of Regulation 22 shall be preserved for a period of two years from the date on which the record was made.

(3) Every requisition, order or prescription (other than a health prescription) on which a controlled drug is supplied in pursuance of these Regulations shall be preserved for a period of two years from the date on which the last delivery under it was made.

Preservation of records relating to drugs in Schedules 3 and 5

24.—(1) A producer of any drug specified in Schedule 3 or 5 and a wholesale dealer in any such drug shall keep every invoice or other like record issued in respect of each quantity of such a drug obtained by him and in respect of each quantity of such a drug supplied by him.

(2) A person who is authorised under Regulation 9(4)*(a)* to supply any drug specified in Schedule 3 shall keep every invoice or other like record issued in respect of each quantity of such a drug obtained by him and in respect of each quantity of such a drug supplied by him.

(3) A retail dealer in any drug specified in Schedule 3, a person in charge or acting person in charge of a hospital or nursing home and a person in charge of a laboratory shall keep every invoice or other like record issued in respect of each quantity of such a drug obtained by him and in respect of each quantity of such a drug supplied by him.

(4) A retail dealer in any drug specified in Schedule 5 shall keep every invoice or other like record issued in respect of each quantity of such a drug obtained by him.

(5) Every invoice or other record which is required by this Regulation to be kept in respect of a drug specified in Schedule 3 shall contain information sufficient to identify the date of the transaction and the person by whom or to whom the drug was supplied.

(6) Every document kept in pursuance of this Regulation (other than a health prescription) shall be preserved for a period of two years from the date on which it is issued:

Provided that the keeping of a copy of the document made at any time during the said period of two years shall be treated for the purposes of this paragraph as if it were the keeping of the original document.

Furnishing of information with respect to controlled drugs

25.—(1) The persons specified in paragraph (2) shall on demand made by the Secretary of State or by any person authorised in writing by the Secretary of State in that behalf:

 (a) furnish such particulars as may be requested in respect of the producing, obtaining or supplying by him of any controlled drug or in respect of any stock of such drugs in his possession;

 (b) for the purpose of confirming any such particulars, produce any stock of such drugs in his possession;

 (c) produce any register, book or document required to be kept under these Regulations relating to any dealings in controlled drugs which is in his possession.

(2) The persons referred to in paragraph (1) are:

 (a) any person authorised by or under these Regulations to produce any controlled drug;

 (b) any person authorised by or under any provision of the Act to import or export any controlled drug;

 (c) a wholesale dealer;

 (d) a retail dealer;

 (e) a practitioner;

 (f) the person in charge or acting person in charge of a hospital or nursing home;

 (g) a person who is in charge of a laboratory;

 (h) a person who is authorised under Regulation 9(4)(a) to supply any controlled drug.

(3) Nothing in this Regulation shall require the furnishing of personal records which a person has acquired or created in the course of his profession or occupation and which he holds in confidence; and in this paragraph "personal records" means documentary and other records concerning an individual (whether living or dead) who can be identified from them and relating to his physical or mental health.

Destruction of controlled drugs

26.—(1) No person who is required by any provision of, or by any term or condition of a licence having effect under, these Regulations to keep records with respect to a drug specified in Schedule 1, 2, 3 or 4 shall destroy such a drug or cause such a drug to be destroyed except in the presence of and in accordance with any directions given by a person authorised (whether personally or as a member of a class) for the purposes of this paragraph by the Secretary of State (hereafter in this Regulation referred to as an "authorised person").

(2) An authorised person may, for the purposes of analysis, take a sample of a drug specified in Schedule 1, 2, 3 or 4 which is to be destroyed.

(3) Where a drug specified in Schedule 1, 2, 3 or 4 is destroyed in pursuance of paragraph (1) by or at the instance of a person who is required by any provision of, or by any term or condition of a licence having effect under, these Regulations to keep a record in respect of the obtaining or supply of that drug, that record shall include particulars of the date of destruction and the quantity destroyed and shall be signed by the authorised person in whose presence the drug is destroyed.

(4) Where the master or owner of a ship or installation manager of an offshore installation has in his possession a drug specified in Schedule 2 which he no longer requires, he shall not destroy the drug or cause it to be destroyed but shall dispose of it to a constable, or to a person who may lawfully supply that drug to him.

(5) Nothing in paragraph (1) or (3) shall apply to any person who is required to keep records only by virtue or Regulation 22(2) or (3) or 24(3).

(6) Nothing in paragraph (1) or (3) shall apply to the destruction of a drug which has been supplied to a practitioner or pharmacist for that purpose in pursuance of Regulation 6(2) or (3).

Revocations

27.—(1) The Regulations specified in Schedule 7 are hereby revoked.

(2) Notwithstanding paragraph (1), any register, record, book, prescription or other document required to be preserved under Regulation 22 or 23 of the Misuse of Drugs Regulations 1973 shall be preserved for the same period of time as if these Regulations had not been made.

(3) In the case of prescription issued before the coming into operation of these Regulations, Regulation 16(1) shall have effect as if:

(a) in the case of prescription containing a controlled drug other than a drug to which the provisions of Regulation 15 of the said Regulations of 1973 applied at the time the prescription was issued, sub-paragraphs *(a)* and *(b)* of that paragraph were omitted; and

(b) in any other case, for the said sub-paragraphs *(a)* and *(b)* there were substituted the words "unless the prescription complies with the provisions of the Misuse of Drugs Regulations 1973 relating to prescriptions".

SCHEDULE 1   Regulation 3

CONTROLLED DRUGS SUBJECT TO THE REQUIREMENTS OF
REGULATIONS 14, 15, 16, 18, 19, 20, 23, 25 and 26.

1. The following substances and products, namely:

(a) Bufotenine
     Cannabinol
     Cannabinol derivatives
     Cannabis and cannabis resin
     [Cathinone][5]
     Coca leaf
     Concentrate of poppy-straw
     Eticyclidine
     Lysergamide
     Lysergide and other *N*-alkyl derivatives of lysergamide
     Mescaline
     Psilocin
     Raw opium
     Rolicyclidine
     Tenocyclidine

5   Added by S.I. 1986/2330 from 1 April 1987.

4-Bromo-2,5-dimethoxy-α-methylphenethylamine
N,N-Diethyltryptamine
N,N-Dimethyltryptamine
2,5-Dimethoxy-α,4-dimethylphenethylamine

(b) any compound (not being a compound for the time being specified in sub-paragraph *(a)* above) structurally derived from tryptamine or from a ring-hydroxy tryptamine by substitution at the nitrogen atom of the sidechain with one or more alkyl substituents but no other substituent;

(c) any compound (not being methoxyphenamine or a compound for the time being specified in sub-paragraph *(a)* above) structurally derived from phenethylamine, an N-alkylphenethylamine, α-methylphenethyl-amine, a N-alkyl-α-methylphenethylamine,α-ethylphenethylamine, or an N-alkyl-αethylphenethylamine by substitution in the ring to any extent with alkyl, alkoxy, alkylenedioxy or halide substituents, whether or not further substituted in the ring by one or more other univalent substituents.

[(d) any compound (not being a compound for the time being specified in Schedule 2) structurally derived from fentanyl by modification in any of the following ways, that is to say,

    (i) by replacement of the phenyl portion of the phenethyl group by any heteromonocycle whether or not further substituted in the hetero-cycle;

    (ii) by substitution in the phenethyl group with alkyl, alkenyl, alkoxy, hydroxy, halogeno, haloalkyl, amino or nitro groups;

    (iii) by substitution in the piperidine ring with alkyl or alkenyl groups;

    (iv) by substitution in the aniline ring with alkyl, alkoxy, alkylenedioxy, halogeno or haloalkyl groups;

    (v) by substitution at the 4-position of the piperidine ring with any alkoxycarbonyl or alkoxyalkyl or acyloxy group;

    (vi) by replacement of the N-propionyl group by another acyl group;

(e) any compound (not being a compound for the time being specified in Schedule 2) structurally derived from pethidine by modification in any of the following ways, that is to say,

    (i) by replacement of the 1-methyl group by an acyl, alkyl whether or not unsaturated, benzyl or phenethyl group, whether or not further substituted;

    (ii) by substitution in the piperidine ring with alkyl or alkenyl groups or with a propano bridge, whether or not further substituted;

    (iii) by substitution in the 4-phenyl ring with alkyl, alkoxy, aryloxy, halogeno or haloalkyl groups;

    (iv) by replacement of the 4-ethoxycarbonyl by any other alkoxy-carbonyl or any alkoxyalkyl or acyloxy group;

    (v) by formation of an N-oxide or of a quaternary base.][5]

2. Any stereoisomeric form of a substance specified in paragraph 1.
3. Any ester or ether of a substance specified in paragraph 1 or 2.
4. Any salt of a substance specified in any of paragraphs 1 to 3.
5. Any preparation or other product containing a substance or product specified in any of paragraphs 1 to 4, not being a preparation specified in Schedule 5.

5 Added by S.I. 1986/2330 from 1 April 1987.

(as amended by S.I. 1986/2330)

CONTROLLED DRUGS SUBJECT TO THE REQUIREMENTS OF
REGULATIONS 14, 15, 16, 18, 19, 20, 21, 23, 25 and 26.

1. The following substances and products, namely:

Acetorphine
Alfentanil
Allylprodine
Alphacetylmethadol
Alphameprodine
Alphamethadol
Alphaprodine
Anileridine
Benzethidine
Benzylmorphine (3-benzylmorphine)
Betacetylmethadol
Betameprodine
Betamethadol
Betaprodine
Bezitramide
[Carfentanil]⁵
Clonitazene
Cocaine
Desomorphine
Dextromoramide
Diamorphine
Diampromide
Diethylthiambutene
Difenoxin
Dihydrocodeinone
    O-carboxymethyloxime
Dihydromorphine
Dimenoxadole
Dimepheptanol
Dimethylthiambutene
Dioxaphetyl butyrate
Diphenoxylate
Dipipanone
Drotebanol
Ecgonine, and any derivative of
    ecgonine which is convertible to
    ecgonine or to cocaine

Ethylmethylthiambutene
Etonitazene
Etorphine
Etoxeridine
Fentanyl
Furethidine
Hydrocodone
Hydromorphinol
Hydromorphone
Hydroxypethidine
Isomethadone
Ketobemidone
Levomethorphan
Levomoramide
Levophenacylmorphan
Levorphanol
[Lofentanil]⁵
Medicinal opium
Metazocine
Methadone
Methadyl acetate
Methyldesorphine
Methyldihydromorphine (6-methyl-
    dihydromorphine)
Metopon
Morpheridine
Morphine
Morphine methobromide, morphine
    N-oxide and other pentavalent
    nitrogen morphine derivatives
Myrophine
Nicomorphine
Noracymethadol
Norlevorphanol
Normethadone
Normorphine
Norpipanone

5   Added by S.I. 1986/2330 from 1 April 1987.

Oxycodone
Oxymorphone
Pethidine
Phenadoxone
Phenampromide
Phenazocine
Phencyclidine
Phenomorphan
Phenorperidine
Piminodine
Piritramide
Proheptazine
Properidine .
Racemethorphan
Racemoramide

Racemorphan
Sufentanil
Thebacon
Thebaine
Tilidate
Trimeperidine
4-Cyano-2-dimethylamino-
4,4-diphenylbutane
4-Cyano-1-methyl-4-phenylpiperidine
1-Methyl-4-phenylpiperidine-
4-carboxylic acid
2-Methyl-3-morpholino-1,1-
diphenylpropanecarboxylic acid
4-Phenylpiperidine-4-carboxylic acid
ethyl ester

2. Any stereoisomeric form of a substance specified in paragraph 1 not being dextromethorphan or dextrorphan.

3. Any ester or ether or a substance specified in paragraph 1 or 2, not being a substance specified in paragraph 6.

4. Any salt of a substance specified in any of paragraphs 1 to 3.

5. Any preparation or other product containing a substance or product specified in any of paragraphs 1 to 4, not being a preparation specified in Schedule 5.

6. The following substances and products, namely:

Acetyldihydrocodeine
Amphetamine
Codeine
Dextropropoxphene
Dihydrocodeine
Ethylmorphine (3-ethylmorphine)
[Fenethylline][5]
[Glutethimide][5]
[Lefetamine][5]
Mecloqualone

Methaqualone
Methylamphetamine
Methylphenidate
Nicocodine
Nicodicodine (6-nicotinoylno-
dihydrocodeine)
Norcodeine
Phenmetrazine
Pholcodine
Propiram

7. Any stereoisomeric form of a substance specified in paragraph 6.

8. Any salt of a substance specified in paragraph 6 or 7.

9. Any preparation or other product containing a substance or product specified in any of paragraphs 6 to 8, not being a preparation specified in Schedule 5.

5   Added by S.I. 1986/2330 from 1 April 1987.

CONTROLLED DRUGS SUBJECT TO THE REQUIREMENTS OF
REGULATIONS 14, 15, 16, 18, 22, 23, 24, 25 and 26.

1. The following substances, namely:

(a) Benzphetamine   Meprobamate
     [Cathine][5]   Methylphenobarbitone
     Chlorphentermine   Methyprylone
     Diethylpropion   Pentazocine
     Ethchlorvynol   Phendimetrazine
     Ethinamate   Phentermine
     Mazindol   Pipradrol
     Mephentermine
(b) any 5,5 disubstituted barbituric acid.

2. Any steroisomeric form of a substance specified in paragraph 1 [not being phenylpropanolamine][5].
3. Any salt of a substance specified in paragraph 1 or 2.
4. Any preparation or other product containing a substance specified in any of paragraphs 1 to 3, not being a preparation specified in Schedule 5.

5. Added by S.I. 1986/2330 from 1 April 1987.

CONTROLLED DRUGS EXCEPTED FROM THE PROHIBITION ON IMPORTATION, EXPORTATION AND, WHEN IN THE FORM OF A MEDICINAL PRODUCT, POSSESSION AND SUBJECT TO THE REQUIREMENTS OF REGULATIONS 22, 23, 25 and 26.

1. The following substances and products, namely:

Alprazolam	Haloxazolam
Bromazepam	Ketazolam
Camazepam	Loprazolam
Chlordiazepoxide	Lorazepam
Clobazam	Lormetazepam
Clonazepam	Medazepam
Clorazepic acid	[Mefenorex][5]
Clotiazepam	Nimetazepam
Cloxazolam	Nitrazepam
Delorazepam	Nordazepam
Diazepam	Oxazepam
Estazolam	Oxazolam
Ethyl loflazepate	Pinazepam
[Fencamfamin][5]	Prazepam
[Fenproporex][5]	[Propylhexedrine][5]
Fludiazepam	[Pyrovalerone][5]
Flunitrazepam	Temazepam
Flurazepam	Tetrazepam
Halazepam	Triazolam
	[N-ethylamphetamine][5]

2. Any steroisomeric form of a substance specified in paragraph 1.
3. Any salt of a substance specified in paragraph 1 or 2.
4. Any preparation or other product containing a substance or product specified in any of paragraphs 1 to 3, not being a preparation specified in Schedule 5.

5   Added by S.I. 1986/2330 from 1 April 1987.

CONTROLLED DRUGS EXCEPTED FROM THE PROHIBITION ON IMPORTATION, EXPORTATION AND POSSESSION AND SUBJECT TO THE REQUIREMENTS OF REGULATIONS 24 and 25.

1.—(1) Any preparation of one or more of the substances to which this paragraph applies, not being a preparation designed for administration by injection, when compounded with one or more other active or inert ingredients and containing a total or not more than 100 milligrammes of the substance or substances (calculated as base) per dosage unit or with a total concentration of not more than 2.5 per cent. (calculated as base) in undivided preparations.

(2) The substances to which this paragraph applies are acetyldihydrocodeine, codeine, dihydrocodeine, ethylmorphine, nicocodine, nicodicodine (6-nicotinoyldihydrocodeine), norcodeine, pholcodine and their respective salts.

2. Any preparation of cocaine containing not more than 0.1 per cent. of cocaine calculated as cocaine base, being a preparation compounded with one or more other active or inert ingredients in such a way that the cocaine cannot be recovered by readily applicable means or in a yield which would constitute a risk to health.

3. Any preparation of medicinal opium or of morphine containing (in either case) not more than 0.2 per cent. of morphine calculated as anhydrous morphine base, being a preparation compounded with one or more other active or inert ingredients in such a way that the opium or, as the case may be, the morphine, cannot be recovered by readily applicable means or in a yield which would constitute a risk to health.

4. Any preparation of dextropropoxphene, being a preparation designed for oral administration containing not more than 135 milligrammes of dextropropoxyphene (calculated as base) per dosage unit or with a total concentration of not more than 2.5 per cent. (calculated as base) in undivided preparations.

5. Any preparation of difenoxin containing, per dosage unit, not more than 0.5 milligrammes of difenoxin and a quantity of atropine sulphate equivalent to at least 5 per cent. of the dose of difenoxin.

6. Any preparation of diphenoxylate containing, per dosage unit, not more than 2.5 milligrammes of diphenoxylate caluculated as base, and a quantity of atropine sulphate equivalent to at least 1 per cent. of the dose of diphenoxylate.

7. Any preparation of propiram containing, per dosage unit, not more than 100 milligrammes of propiram calculated as base and compounded with at least the same amount (by weight) of methylcellulose.

8. Any powder of ipecacuanha and opium comprising:

   10 per cent. opium, in powder,
   10 per cent. ipecacuanha root, in powder, well mixed with
   80 per cent. of any other powdered ingredient containing no controlled drug.

9. Any mixture containing one or more of the preparations specified in paragraphs 1 to 8, being a mixture of which none of the other ingredients is a controlled drug.

Regulation 3   SCHEDULE 6

Regulation 3

FORM OF REGISTER

PART I

Entries to be made in case of obtaining

Date on which supply received	NAME Of person or firm from whom obtained	ADDRESS	Amount obtained	Form in which obtained

PART II

Entries to be made in case of supply

Date on which the transaction was effected	NAME Of person or firm supplied	ADDRESS	Particulars as to licence or authority of person or firm supplied to be in possession	Amount supplied	Form in which supplied

Regulation 27   SCHEDULE 7

REGULATIONS REVOKED

Column 1 Regulations Revoked	Column 2 References
The Misuse of Drugs Regulations 1973	S.I. 1973/797
The Misuse of Drugs (Amendment) Regulations 1974	S.I. 1974/402
The Misuse of Drugs (Amendment) Regulations 1975	S.I. 1975/499
The Misuse of Drugs (Amendment) Regulations 1977	S.I. 1977/1380
The Misuse of Drugs (Amendment) Regulations 1979	S.I. 1979/326
The Misuse of Drugs (Amendment) Regulations 1983	S.I. 1983/788
The Misuse of Drugs (Amendment) Regulations 1984	S.I. 1984/1143

The Misuse of Drugs (Safe Custody) (Amendment) Regulations 1985 and 1986

(S.I. 1985 No. 2067 and 1986 No. 2332)

The Misuse of Drugs (Safe Custody) (Amendment) Regulations 1985 (S.I. No. 2067) make certain amendments to the Safe Custody Regulations with effect from 1 April 1986.

The Misuse of Drugs (Safe Custody) (Amendment) Regulations 1985
(S.I. No. 2067)

Made - - - - -	*19th December 1985*
Laid before Parliament	*15th January 1986*
Coming into Operation	*1st April 1986*

1. These Regulations may be cited as the Misuse of Drugs (Safe Custody) (Amendment) Regulations 1985 and shall come into operation on 1st April 1986.

2.—(1) Schedule 1 to the Misuse of Drugs (Safe Custody) Regulations 1973[1] shall be amended in accordance with the following provisions of this Regulation.

(2) For paragraph 1 there shall be substituted the following paragraph:

"1. Any controlled drug specified in Schedule 4 or 5 to the Misuse of Drugs Regulations 1985".[2]

(3) After paragraph 3 there shall be inserted the following paragraph:

"**4.** Any of the following substances and products, that is to say:

(a) Ethchlorvynol

(b) Ethinamate

(c) Mazindol

(d) Meprobamate

(e) Methyprylone

(f) Pentazocine

(g) Phentermine

(h) Any stereoisomeric form of a substance specified in any of paragraphs *(a)* to *(g)* above.

(i) Any salt of a substance specified in any of paragraphs *(a)* to *(h)* above.

(j) Any preparation or other product containing a substance or product specified in any of paragraphs *(a)* to *(i)* above.".

---

1 S.I. 1973/798, as amended by S.I. 1974/1449, 1975/294, 1984/1146. See Appendix V of main work.
2 S.I. 1985/2066. Reproduced in Appendix IV of this supplement.

S.I. 1986/2332 made further amendments with effect from 1 April 1987 as follows.

The Misuse of Drugs (Safe Custody) (Amendment) Regulations 1986
(S.I. No. 2332)

Made - - - - -	*22nd December 1986*
Laid before Parliament	*13th January 1987*
Coming into Operation	*1st April 1987*

1. These Regulations may be cited as the Misuse of Drugs (Safe Custody) (Amendment) Regulations 1986 and shall come into operation on 1st April 1987.

2. For Schedule 1 to the Misuse of Drugs (Safe Custody) Regulations 1973[3] there shall be substituted the following Schedule:

"SCHEDULE 1

EXEMPTED DRUGS

1. Any controlled drug specified in Schedule 4 or 5 to the Misuse of Drugs Regulations 1985.[4]

2. Any liquid preparation designed for administration otherwise than by injection which contains any of the following substances and products, this is to say:

(a) Amphetamine

(b) Benzphetamine

(c) Chlorphentermine

(d) Fenethylline

(e) Mephentermine

(f) Methaqualone

(g) Methylamphetamine

(h) Methylphenidate

(i) Phendimetrazine

(j) Phenmetrazine

(k) Pipradrol

(l) Any stereoisomeric form of a substance specified in any of paragraphs *(a)* to *(k)* above.

(m) Any salt of a substance specified in any of paragraphs *(a)* to *(l)* above.

3. Any of the following substances and products, that is to say:

(a) Any 5,5 disubstituted barbituric acid

(b) Cathine

(c) Ethchlorvynol

(d) Ethinamate

(e) Mazindol

---

3 S.I. 1973/798; Schedule 1 was amended by S.I. 1984/1146 and 1985/2067. See Appendix V of main work.

4 S.I. 1985/2066. Reproduced in Appendix IV of this supplement.

96

(f) Meprobamate
(g) Methylphenobarbitone
(h) Methyprylone
(i) Pentazocine
(j) Phentermine
(k) Any stereoisomeric form of a substance specified in any of paragraphs *(a)* to *(j)* above.
(l) Any salt of a substance specified in any of paragraphs *(a)* to *(k)* above.
(m) Any preparation or other product containing a substance or product specified in any of paragraphs *(a)* to *(l)* above.".

The Misuse of Drugs (Designation) Order 1986

(S.I. 1986 No. 2331)

Made - - - - -	*22nd December 1986*
Laid before Parliament	*13th January 1987*
Coming into Operation	*1st April 1987*

1. This Order may be cited as the Misuse of Drugs (Designation) Order 1986 and shall come into operation on 1st April 1987.

2.—(1) The controlled drugs specified in Part I of the Schedule hereto are hereby designated as drugs to which section 7(4) of the Misuse of Drugs Act 1971 applies.

(2) Part II of the Schedule hereto shall have effect for the purpose of specifying those controlled drugs which are excepted from Part I thereof.

3. The Misuse of Drugs (Designation) Order 1977[1] and the Misuse of Drugs (Designation) (Variation) Order 1984[2] are hereby revoked.

SCHEDULE *Article 2*

PART I

CONTROLLED DRUGS TO WHICH SECTION 7(4) OF THE MISUSE OF DRUGS ACT 1971
APPLIES

1. The following substances and products, namely:

(a)
Bufotenine	Lysergide and other *N*-alkyl derivatives
Cannabinol	of lysergamide
Cannabinol derivatives	Mescaline
Cannabis	Psilocin
Cannabis resin	Raw opium
Cathinone	Rolicyclidine
Coca leaf	Tenocyclidine
Concentrate of poppy-straw	4-Bromo-2, 5-dimethoxy-α-methyl-
Eticyclidine	phenethylamine
Lysergamide	*N, N*-Diethyltryptamine
	N, N-Dimethyltryptamine
	2,5-Dimethoxy-α, 4-dimethyl-
	phenethylamine

(b) any compound (not being a compound for the time being specified in subparagraph *(a)* above) structurally derived from tryptamine or from a ring-hydroxy tryptamine by substitution at the nitrogen atom of the sidechain with one or more alkyl substituents but no other substituent;

1 S.I. 1977/1379.
2 S.I. 1984/1144.

(c) any compound (not being methoxyphenamine or a compound for the time being specified in sub-paragraph *(a)* above) structurally derived from phenethylamine, an *N*-alkylphenethylamine, α-methylphenethylamine, an *N*-alkyl-α-methylphenethylamine, α-ethylphenethylamine, or an *N*-alkyl-α-ethylphenethylamine by substitution in the ring to any extent with alkyl, alkoxy, alkylenedioxy or halide substituents, whether or not further substituted in the ring by one or more other univalent substituents;

(d) any compound (not be a compound for the time being specified in Part II of this Schedule) structurally derived from fentanyl by modification in any of the following ways, that is to say,

(i) by replacement of the phenyl portion of the phenethyl group by any heteromonocycle whether or not further substituted in the heterocycle;

(ii) by substitution in the phenethyl group with alkyl, alkenyl, alkoxy, hydroxy, halogeno, haloalkyl, amino or nitro groups;

(iii) by substitution in the piperidine ring with alkyl or alkenyl groups;

(iv) by substitution in the aniline ring with alkyl, alkoxy, alkylenedioxy, halogeno or haloalkyl groups;

(v) by substitution at the 4-position of the piperidine ring with any alkoxycarbonyl or alkoxyalkyl or acyloxy group;

(vi) by replacement of the *N*-propionyl group by another acyl group;

(e) any compound (not being a compound for the time being specified in Part II of this Schedule) that is structurally derived from pethidine by modification in any of the following ways, that is to say,

(i) by replacement of the 1-methyl group by an acyl, alkyl whether or not unsaturated, benzyl or phenethyl group, whether or not further substituted;

(ii) by substitution in the piperidine ring with alkyl or alkenyl groups or with a propano bridge, whether or not further substituted;

(iii) by substitution in the 4-phenyl ring with alkyl, alkoxy, aryloxy, halogeno or haloalkyl groups;

(iv) by replacement of the 4-ethoxycarbonyl by any other alkoxycarbonyl or any alkoxyalkyl or acyloxy group;

(v) by formation of an *N*-oxide or of a quaternary base.

2. Any stereoisomeric form of a substance specified in paragraph 1 above.

3. Any ester or ether of a substance specified in paragraph 1 or 2 above.

4. Any salt of a substance specified in any of paragraphs 1 to 3 above.

5. Any preparation or other product containing a substance or product specified in any of paragraphs 1 to 4 above.

PART II

CONTROLLED DRUGS EXCEPTED FROM PART I

1. The compounds referred to in paragraph 1*(d)* of Part I of this Schedule are:
Alfentanil
Carfentanil
Lofentanil
Sufentanil.

2. The compounds referred to in paragraph 1(e) of Part I of this Schedule are:
   Allyprodine
   Alphameprodine
   Alphaprodine
   Anileridine
   Betameprodine
   Betaprodine
   Hydroxypethidine
   Properidine
   Timeperidine.

Police and Criminal Evidence Act 1984

Sections 29(1), 32 and 36 of the Drug Trafficking Offences Act 1986 amend sections of the Act and are in the following terms.

29.—(1) For the purposes of section 21 and 22 of the Police and Criminal Evidence Act 1984 (access to, and copying and retention of, seized material):

(a) an investigation into drug trafficking shall be treated as if it were an investigation of or in connection with an offence, and

(b) material produced in pursuance of an order under section 27(2)(a) of this Act shall be treated as if it were material seized by a constable.

Authorisation of delay in notifying arrest.

32.—(1) In section 56 of the Police and Criminal Evidence Act 1984 (right to have someone informed when arrested), at the beginning of subsection (5) there is inserted "Subject to subsection (5A) below" and after that subsection there is inserted:

"5(A) An officer may also authorise delay where the serious arrestable offence is a drug trafficking offence and the officer has reasonable grounds for believing:

(a) that the detained person has benefited from drug trafficking, and

(b) that the recovery of the value of that person's proceeds of drug trafficking will be hindered by telling the named person of the arrest."

(2) In section 58 of that Act (access to legal advice) at the beginning of subsection (8) there is inserted "Subject to subsection (8A) below" and after that subsection there is inserted:

"(8A) An officer may also authorise delay where the serious arrestable offence is a drug trafficking offence and the officer has reasonable grounds for believing:

(a) that the detained person has benefited from drug trafficking, and

(b) that the recovery of the value of that person's proceeds of drug trafficking will be hindered by the exercise of the right conferred by subsection (1) above."

(3) In section 65 of that Act (interpretation):

(a) after the definition of "appropriate consent" there is inserted:
"drug trafficking" and "drug trafficking offence" have the same meaning as in the Drug Trafficking Offences Act 1986", and

(b) at the end of that section there is inserted "and references in this Part to any person's proceeds of drug trafficking are to be construed in accordance with the Drug Trafficking Offences Act 1986".

(4) Without prejudice to section 20(2) of the Interpretation Act 1978, the Police and Criminal Evidence Act 1984 (Application to Customs and Excise) Order 1985 applies to sections 56 and 58 of the Police and Criminal Evidence Act 1984 as those sections have effect by virtue of this section.

Section 116(2) is amended by section 36 of the Drug Trafficking Offences Act 1986. A new paragraph is added:

"*(aa)* Any of the offences mentioned in paragraphs (a) to (d) of the definition of 'drug trafficking offence' in section 38(1) of the Drug Trafficking Offences Act 1986."

The Police and Criminal Evidence Act 1984 is applied to the Customs and Excise with effect from January 1986 by the following statutory instrument:

The Police and Criminal Evidence Act 1984 (Application to Customs and Excise) Order 1985

(S.I. No. 1800)

Made - - - -	*20th November 1985*
Laid before Parliament	*28th November 1985*
Coming into Operation	*1st January 1986*

1. This Order may be cited as the Police and Criminal Evidence Act 1984 (Application to Customs and Excise) Order 1985 and shall come into operation on 1st January 1986.

2.—(1) In this Order, unless the context otherwise requires:
"the Act" means the Police and Criminal Evidence Act 1984;
"assigned matter" has the meaning given to it by section 1 of the Customs and Excise Management Act 1979;
"the customs and excise Acts" has the meaning given to it by section 1 of the Customs and Excise Management Act 1979;
"customs office" means a place for the time being occupied by Her Majesty's Customs and Excise;
"officer" means a person commissioned by the Commissioners of Customs and Excise under section 6(3) of the Customs and Excise Management Act 1979.
(2) A person is in customs detention for the purpose of this Order if:
(a) he has been taken to a customs office after being arrested for an offence; or
(b) he is arrested at a customs office after attending voluntarily at the office or accompanying an officer to it,
and is detained there or is detained elsewhere in the charge of an officer, and nothing shall prevent a detained person from being transferred between customs detention and police detention.

102

3.—(1) Subject to the modifications in paragraphs (2) and (3) of this article, in articles 4 to 11 below and in Schedule 2 to this Order, the provisions of the Act contained in Schedule 1 to this Order which relate to investigations of offences conducted by police officers or to persons detained by the police shall apply to investigations conducted by officers of Customs and Excise of offences which relate to assigned matters, and to persons detained by such officers.

(2) The Act shall have effect as if the words and phrases in Column 1 or Part 1 of Schedule 2 to this Order were replaced by the substitute words and phrases in Column 2 of that Part.

(3) Where in the Act any act or thing is to be done by a constable of a specified rank, that act or thing shall be done by an officer of at least the grade specified in Column 2 of Part 2 of Schedule 2 to this Order, and the Act shall be interpreted as if the substituted grade were specified in the Act.

4. Nothing in the application of the Act to Customs and Excise shall be construed as conferring upon an officer any power:

(a) to charge a person with any offence;

(b) to release a person on bail;

(c) to detain a person for an offence after he has been charged with that offence.

5.—(1) Where in the Act a constable is given power to seize and retain any thing found upon a lawful search of person or premises, an officer shall have the same power notwithstanding that the thing found is not evidence of an offence in relation to an assigned matter.

(2) Nothing in the application of the Act to Customs and Excise shall be construed to prevent anything lawfully seized by a person under any enactment from being accepted and retained by an officer.

(3) Section 21 of the Act (access and copying) shall not apply to anything seized as liable to forfeiture under the customs and excise Acts.

6. In its application by virtue of article 3 above the Act shall have effect as if the following section were inserted after section 14:

"14A. Material in the possession of a person who acquired or created it in the course of any trade, business, profession or other occupation or for the purpose of any paid or unpaid office and which relates to an assigned matter, as defined in section 1 of the Customs and Excise Management Act 1979, is neither excluded material nor special procedure material for the purposes of any enactment such as is mentioned in section 9(2) above.".

7. Section 18(1) of the Act shall be modified as follows:

"18.—(1) Subject to the following provisions of this section, an officer of Customs and Excise may enter and search any premises occupied or controlled by a person who is under arrest for any arrestable offence which relates to an assigned matter, as defined in section 1 of the Customs and Excise Management Act 1979, if he has reasonable grounds for suspecting that there is on the premises evidence, other than items subject to legal privilege, that relates:

(a) to that offence; or

(b) to some other arrestable offence which is connected with or similar to that offence."

8.—(1) The Commissioners of Customs and Excise shall keep on an annual basis the written records mentioned in subsection (1) of section 50 of the Act.

(2) The Annual Report of the Commissioners of Her Majesty's Customs and Excise shall contain information about the matters mentioned in subsection (1) of section 50 of the Act in respect of the period to which it relates.

9.—(1) Section 55 of the Act shall have effect as if it related only to things such as are mentioned in subsection (1)*(a)* of that section.

(2) The Annual Report of the Commissioners of Her Majesty's Customs and Excise shall contain the information mentioned in subsection (15) of section 55 of the Act about searches made under that section.

10. Section 77(3) of the Act shall be modified to the extent that the definition of "independent person" shall, in addition to the persons mentioned therein, also include an officer or any other person acting under the authority of the Commissioners of Customs and Excise.

11. Where any provision of the Act as applied to Customs and Excise:

(a) confers a power on an officer, and

(b) does not provide that the power may only be excercised with the consent of some person other than an officer,

the officer may use reasonable force, if necessary, in the exercise of the power.

SCHEDULES

SCHEDULE 1   *(Article 3)*

PROVISIONS OF THE ACT APPLIED TO CUSTOMS AND EXCISE

Section 8
Section 9 and Schedule 1
Section 15
Section 16
Section 17(1)*(b)*, (2), (4)
Section 18 subject to the modification in article 7 hereof
Section 19
Section 20
Section 21 subject to the modifications in article 5 hereof
Section 22(1) to (4)
Section 28
Section 29
Section 30(1) to (4)*(a)* and (5) to (11)
Section 31
Section 32(1) to (9) subject to the modifications in article 5 hereof
Section 34(1) to (5)
Section 35
Section 36
Section 37
Section 39
Section 40
Section 41
Section 42
Section 43
Section 44
Section 50 subject to the modification in article 8 hereof
Section 51*(d)*
Section 52
Section 54
Section 55 subject to the modifications in articles 5 and 9 hereof
Section 56(1) to (9)[1]
Section 57(1) to (9)
Section 58(1) to (11)[1]
Section 62
Section 63
Section 64(1) to (6)
[Section 107][2]

---

1   The Order applies to these sections as modified by section 32 of the Drug Trafficking Offences Act 1986 (reproduced earlier in this Appendix).
2   Added by S.I. 1987/439

SCHEDULE 2 (*Article* 3)

PART 1

Substitution of equivalent words and phrases in the Act.

Where in the Act a word or phrase specified in Column 1 below is used, in the application of the Act to Customs and Excise, there shall be substituted the equivalent word or phrase in Column 2 below—

Column 1	Column 2
WORDS AND PHRASES USED IN THE ACT	SUBSTITUTED WORDS AND PHRASES
area	collection
chief officer	collector
constable	officer
designated police station	designated customs office
officer of a force maintained by a police authority	officer
police area	collection
police detention (except in section 118 and in section 39(1)(*a*) the second time the words occur)	customs detention
police force	HM Commissioners of Customs and Excise
police officer	officer
police station	customs office
rank	grade
station	customs office
the police	HM Customs and Excise

PART 2

Equivalent grades of officers.

Where in the Act an act or thing is to be done by a constable of the rank specified in Column 1 below, that same act or thing shall, in the application of the Act to Customs and Excise, be done by an officer of at least the grade specified in Column 2 below—

Column 1	Column 2
RANK OF CONSTABLE	GRADE OR OFFICER
sergeant	executive officer
inspector	higher executive officer
superintendent	senior executive officer
[chief inspector	higher executive officer
chief superintendant	grade 7][3]

3 Added by S.I. 1987/439

106

Police and Criminal Evidence Act 1984

Section 68 and Schedule 3 (not printed in main work)

Evidence from documentary records.

68.—(1) Subject to section 69 below, a statement in a document shall be admissible in any proceedings as evidence of any fact stated therein of which direct oral evidence would be admissible if:

(a) the document is or forms part of a record compiled by a person acting under a duty from information supplied by a person (whether acting under a duty or not) who had, or may reasonably be supposed to have had, personal knowledge of the matters dealt with in that information; and

(b) any condition relating to the person who supplied the information which is specified in subsection (2) below is satisfied.

(2) The conditions mentioned in subsection (1)*(b)* above are:

(a) that the person who supplied the information:

   (i) is dead or by reason of his bodily or mental condition unfit to attend as a witness;

   (ii) is outside the United Kingdom and it is not reasonably practicable to secure his attendance; or

   (iii) cannot reasonably be expected (having regard to the time which has elapsed since he supplied or acquired the information and to all the circumstances) to have any recollection of the matters dealt with in that information;

(b) that all reasonable steps have been taken to identify the person who supplied the information but that he cannot be identified; and

(c) that, the identity of the person who supplied the information being known, all reasonable steps have been taken to find him, but that he cannot be found.

(3) Nothing in this section shall prejudice the admissibility of any evidence that would be admissible apart from this section.

SCHEDULE 3
(Section 70)

PROVISIONS SUPPLEMENTARY TO SECTIONS 68 and 69

PART I

PROVISIONS SUPPLEMENTARY TO SECTION 68

1. Section 68(1) above applies whether the information contained in the document was supplied directly or indirectly but, if it was supplied indirectly, only if each person through whom it was supplied was acting under a duty; and applies also where the person compiling the record is himself the person by whom the information is supplied.

2. Where:

(a) a document setting out the evidence which a person could be expected to give as a witness has been prepared for the purpose of any pending or contemplated proceedings; and

(b) it falls within subsection (1) of section 68 above,

a statement contained in it shall not be given in evidence by virtue of that section without the leave of the court, and the court shall not give leave unless it is of the opinion that the statement ought to be admitted in the interests of justice, having regard:

(i) to the circumstances in which leave is sought and in particular to the contents of the statement; and

(ii) to any likelihood that the accused will be prejudiced by its admission in the absence of the person who supplied the information on which it is based.

3. Where in any proceedings a statement based on information supplied by any person is given in evidence by virtue of section 68 above:

(a) any evidence which, if that person had been called as a witness, would have been admissible as relevant to his credibility as a witness shall be admissible for that purpose in those proceedings;

(b) evidence may, with the leave of the court, be given of any matter which, if that person had been called as a witness, could have been put to him in cross-examination as relevant to his credibility as a witness but of which evidence could not have been adduced by the cross-examining party; and

(c) evidence tending to prove that that person, whether before or after supplying the information, made a statement (whether oral or not) which is inconsistent with it shall be admissible for the purpose of showing that he has contradicted himself.

4. A statement which is admissible by virtue of section 68 above shall not be capable of corroborating evidence given by the person who supplied the information on which the statement is based.

5. In deciding for the purposes of section 68(2)(a)(i) above whether a person is unfit to attend as a witness the court may act on a certificate purporting to be signed by a registered medical practitioner.

6. Any reference in section 68 above or this Part of this Schedule to a person acting under a duty includes a reference to a person acting in the course of any trade, business, profession or other occupation in which he is engaged or employed or for the purposes of any paid or unpaid office held by him.

7. In estimating the weight, if any, to be attached to a statement admissible in evidence by virtue of section 68 above regard shall be had to all the circumstances from which any inference can reasonably be drawn as to the accuracy or otherwise of the statement and, in particular:

(a) to the question whether or not the person who supplied the information from which the record containing the statement was compiled did so contemporaneously with the occurrence or existence of the facts dealt with in that information; and

(b) to the question whether or not that person, or any other person concerned with compiling or keeping the record containing the statement, had any incentive to conceal or misrepresent the facts.

PROVISIONS SUPPLEMENTARY TO SECTION 69

8. In any proceedings where it is desired to give a statement in evidence in accordance with section 69 above, a certificate:

 (a) identifying the document containing the statement and describing the manner in which it was produced;

 (b) giving such particulars of any device involved in the production of that document as may be appropriate for the purpose of showing that the document was produced by a computer;

 (c) dealing with any of the matters mentioned in subsection (1) of section 69 and above; and

 (d) purporting to be signed by a person occupying a responsible position in relation to the operation of the computer,

shall be evidence of anything stated in it; and for the purposes of this paragraph it shall be sufficient for a matter to be stated to the best of the knowledge and belief of the person stating it.

9. Notwithstanding paragraph 8 above, a court may require oral evidence to be given of anything of which evidence could be given by a certificate under that paragraph.

10. Any person who in a certificate tendered under paragraph 8 above in a magistrates' court, the Crown Court or the Court of Appeal makes a statement which he knows to be false or does not believe to be true shall be guilty of an offence and liable:

 (a) on conviction on indictment to imprisonment for a term not exceeding two years or to a fine or to both;

 (b) on summary conviction to imprisonment for a term not exceeding six months or to a fine not exceeding the statutory maximum (as defined in section 74 of the Criminal Justice Act 1982) or to both.

11. In estimating the weight, if any, to be attached to a statement regard shall be had to all the circumstances from which any inference can reasonably be drawn as to the accuracy or otherwise of the statement and, in particular:

 (a) to the question whether or not the information which the information contained in the statement reproduces or is derived from was supplied to the relevant computer, or recorded for the purpose of being supplied to it, contemporaneously with the occurrence or existence of the facts dealt with in that information; and

 (b) to the question whether or not any person concerned with the supply of information to that computer, or with the operation of that computer or any equipment by means of which the document containing the statement was produced by it, had any incentive to conceal or misrepresent the facts.

12. For the purposes of paragraph 11 above information shall be taken to be supplied to a computer whether it is supplied directly or (with or without human intervention) by means of any appropriate equipment.

PART III

PROVISIONS SUPPLEMENTARY TO SECTIONS 68 and 69

13. Where in any proceedings a statement contained in a document is admissible in evidence by virtue of section 68 above or in accordance with section 69 above it may be proved:

  (a) by the production of that document; or
  (b) (whether or not that document is still in existence) by the production of a copy of that document, or of the material part of it,

authenticated in such manner as the court may approve.

14. For the purpose of deciding whether or not a statement is so admissible the court may draw any reasonable inference:

  (a) from the circumstances in which the statement was made or otherwise came into being; or
  (b) from any other circumstances, including the form and contents of the document in which the statement is contained.

15. Provision may be made by rules of court for supplementing the provisions of section 68 or 69 above or this Schedule.

Misuse of Drugs Act 1971 (Modification) Order 1985

This order was made on 18 December 1985 in the form printed in the corresponding appendix of the main work. The S.I. No. is 1985/1995. The effect of the order in its application to benzodiazines is limited by Schedule 4 of the Misuse of Drugs Regulations 1985 (set out in Appendix IV to this supplement).

Drug Trafficking Offences Act 1986

(CHAPTER 32)

ARRANGEMENT OF SECTIONS

Confiscation of proceeds of drug trafficking

Confiscation of proceeds of drug trafficking

Confiscation orders.

1.—(1) Subject to subsection (7) below, where a person appears before the Crown Court to be sentenced in respect of one or more drug trafficking offences (and has not previously been sentenced or otherwise dealt with in respect of his conviction for the offence or, as the case may be, any of the offences concerned), the court shall act as follows.

(2) The court shall first determine whether he has benefited from drug trafficking.

(3) For the purposes of this Act, a person who has at any time (whether before or after the commencement of this section) received any payment or other reward in connection with drug trafficking carried on by him or another has benefited from drug trafficking.

(4) If the court determines that he has so benefited, the court shall, before sentencing or otherwise dealing with him in respect of the offence or, as the case may be, any of the offences concerned, determine in accordance with section 4 of this Act the amount to be recovered in his case by virtue of this section.

(5) The court shall then, in respect of the offence or offences concerned:

(a) order him to pay that amount,
(b) take account of the order before:
(i) imposing any fine on him, or
(ii) making any order involving any payment by him, or

113

(iii) making any order under section 27 of the Misuse of Drugs Act 1971 (forfeiture orders), section 39 of the Powers of Criminal Courts Act 1973 (criminal bankruptcy orders) or section 43 of that Act (deprivation orders), and

(c) subject to paragraph (b) above, leave the order out of account in determining the appropriate sentence or other manner of dealing with the defendant.

(6) No enactment restricting the power of a court dealing with an offender in a particular way from dealing with him also in any other way shall by reason only of the making of an order under this section restrict the Crown Court from dealing with an offender in any way the court considers appropriate in respect of a drug trafficking offence.

(7) Subsection (1) above does not apply in relation to any offence for which a person appears before the Crown Court to be sentenced if:

(a) he has been committed to the Crown Court for sentence in respect of that offence under section 37(1) of the Magistrates' Courts Act 1980 (committal to Crown Court with a view to sentence of youth custody), or

(b) the powers of the court (apart from this section) to deal with him in respect of that offence are limited to dealing with him in any way in which a magistrates' court might have dealt with him in respect of the offence.

(8) In this Act:

(a) an order under this section is referred to as a "confiscation order", and

(b) a person against whom proceedings have been instituted for a drug trafficking offence is referred to (whether or not he has been convicted) as "the defendant".

Assessing the proceeds of drug trafficking.

2.—(1) For the purposes of this Act:

(a) any payments or other rewards received by a person at any time (whether before or after the commencement of section 1 of this Act) in connection with drug trafficking carried on by him or another are his proceeds of drug trafficking, and

(b) the value of his proceeds of drug trafficking in the aggregate of the values of the payments or other rewards.

(2) The Court may, for the purpose of determining whether the defendant has benefited from drug trafficking and, if he has, of assessing the value of his proceeds of drug trafficking, make the following assumptions, except to the extent that any of the assumptions are shown to be incorrect in the defendant's case.

(3) Those assumptions are:

(a) that any property appearing to the court:
   (i) to have been held by him at any time since his conviction, or
   (ii) to have been transferred to him at any time since the beginning of the period of six years ending when the proceedings were instituted against him.
   was received by him, at the earliest time at which he appears to the court to have held it, as a payment or reward in connection with drug trafficking carried on by him,

114

(b) that any expenditure of his since the beginning of that period was met out of payments received by him in connection with drug trafficking carried on by him, and

(c) that, for the purpose of valuing any property received or assumed to have been received by him at any time as such a reward, he received the property free of any other interests in it.

(4) Subsection (2) above does not apply if the only drug trafficking offence in respect of which the defendant appears before the court to be sentenced is an offence under section 24 of this Act.

(5) For the purpose of assessing the value of the defendant's proceeds of drug trafficking in a case where a confiscation order has previously been made against him, the court shall leave out of account any of his proceeds of drug trafficking that are shown to the court to have been taken into account in determining the amount to be recovered under that order.

Statements relating to drug trafficking.

3.—(1) Where:

(a) there is tendered to the Crown Court by the prosecutor a statement as to any matters relevant to the determination whether the defendant has benefited from drug trafficking or to the assessment of the value of his proceeds of drug trafficking, and

(b) the defendant accepts to any extent any allegation in the statement,

the court may, for the purposes of that determination and assessment, treat his acceptance as conclusive of the matters to which it relates.

(2) Where:

(a) a statement is tendered under subsection (1)*(a)* above, and

(b) the court is satisfied that a copy of that statement has been served on the defendant,

the court may require the defendant to indicate to what extent he accepts each allegation in the statement and, so far as he does not accept any such allegation, to indicate any matters he proposes to rely on.

(3) If the defendant fails in any respect to comply with a requirement under subsection (2) above he may be treated for the purposes of this section as accepting every allegation in the statement apart from:

(a) any allegation in respect of which he has complied with the requirement, and

(b) any allegation that he has benefited from drug trafficking or that any payment or other reward was received by him in connection with drug trafficking carried on by him or another.

(4) Where:

(a) there is tendered to the Crown Court by the defendant a statement as to any matters relevant to determining the amount that might be realised at the time the confiscation order is made, and

(b) the prosecutor accepts to any extent any allegation in the statement,

the court may, for the purposes of that determination, treat the acceptance by the prosecutor as conclusive of the matters to which it relates.

115

(5) An allegation may be accepted or a matter indicated for the purposes of this section either:

  (a) orally before the court, or
  (b) in writing in accordance with Crown Court Rules.

(6) No acceptance by the defendant under this section that any payment or other reward was received by him in connection with drug trafficking carried on by him or another shall be admissible in evidence in any proceedings for an offence.

Amount to be recovered under confiscation order

4.—(1) Subject to subsection (3), below, the amount to be recovered in the defendant's case under the confiscation order shall be the amount the Crown Court assesses to be the value of the defendant's proceeds of drug trafficking.

(2) If the court is satisfied as to any matter relevant for determining the amount that might be realised at the time the confiscation order is made (whether by an acceptance under section 3 of this Act or otherwise), the court may issue a certificate giving the court's opinion as to the matters concerned and shall do so if satisfied as mentioned in subsection (3) below.

(3) If the court is satisfied that the amount that might be realised at the time the confiscation order is made is less than the amount the court assesses to be the value of his proceeds of drug trafficking, the amount to be recovered in the defendant's case under the confiscation order shall be the amount appearing to the court to be the amount that might be so realised.

Definition of principal terms used

5.—(1) In this Act, "realisable property" means, subject to subsection (2) below:

  (a) any property held by the defendant, and
  (b) any property held by a person to whom the defendant has directly or indirectly made a gift caught by this Act.

(2) Property is not realisable property if:

  (a) an order under section 43 of the Powers of Criminal Courts Act 1973 (deprivation orders),
  (b) an order under section 27 of the Misuse of Drugs Act 1971 (forfeiture orders), or
  (c) an order under section 223 or 436 of the Criminal Procedure (Scotland) Act 1975 (forfeiture of property),

is in force in respect of the property.

(3) For the purposes of sections 3 and 4 of this Act the amount that might be realised at the time a confiscation order is made against the defendant is:

  (a) the total of the values at that time of all the realisable property held by the defendant, less
  (b) where there are obligations having priority at that time, the total amounts payable in pursuance of such obligations,

together with the total of the values at that time of all gifts caught by this Act.

116

(4) Subject to the following provisions of this section, for the purposes of this Act the value of property (other than cash) in relation to any person holding the property:

(a) where any other person holds an interest in the property, is:
  (i) the market value of the first mentioned person's beneficial interest in the property, less
  (ii) the amount required to discharge any incumbrance (other than a charging order) on that interest, and

(b) in any other case, is its market value,

(5) Subject to subsection (10) below, references in this Act to the value at any time (referred to in subsection (6) below as "the material time") of a gift caught by this Act or of any payment or reward are references to:

(a) the value of the gift, payment or reward to the recipient when he received it adjusted to take account of subsequent changes in the value of money, or

(b) where subsection (6) below applies, the value there mentioned,

whichever is the greater.

(6) Subject to subsection (10) below, if at the material time the recipient holds:

(a) the property which he received (not being cash), or

(b) property which, in whole or in part, directly or indirectly represents in his hands the property which he received.

the value referred to in subsection (5)(b) above is the value to him at the material time of the property mentioned in paragraph (a) above or, as the case may be, of the property mentioned in paragraph (b) above so far as it so represents the property which he received, but disregarding in either case any charging order.

(7) For the purposes of subsection (3) above, an obligation has priority at any time if it is an obligation of the defendant to:

(a) pay an amount due in respect of a fine, or other order of a court, imposed or made on conviction of an offence, where the fine was imposed or order made before the confiscation order, or

(b) pay any sum which would be included among the preferential debts (within the meaning given by section 386 of the Insolvency Act 1986) in the defendant's bankruptcy commencing on the date of the confiscation order or winding up under an order of the court made on that date.

(8) In the case of a confiscation order made before the coming into force of the Insolvency Act 1986, subsection (7) above shall have effect as if for paragraph (b) there were substituted:

"(b) pay any sum which, if the defendant had been adjudged bankrupt or was being wound up, would be among the preferential debts.";

and in that paragraph "the preferential debts":

(a) in relation to bankruptcy, means the debts to be paid in priority under section 33 of the Bankruptcy Act 1914 (assuming the date of the confiscation order to be the date of the receiving order) and

(b) in relation to winding up, means the preferential debts listed in Schedule 19 to the Companies Act 1985 (assuming the date of the confiscation order to be relevant date for the purpose of that Schedule).

117

(9) A gift (including a gift made before the commencement of section 1 of this Act) is caught by this Act if:

(a) it was made by the defendant at any time since the beginning of the period of six years ending when the proceedings were instituted against him, or

(b) it was made by the defendant at any time and was a gift of property:
   (i) received by the defendant in connection with drug trafficking carried on by him or another, or
   (ii) which in whole or in part directly or indirectly represented in the defendant's hands property received by him in that connection.

(10) For the purposes of this Act:

(a) the circumstances in which the defendant is to be treated as making a gift include those where he transfers property to another person directly or indirectly for a consideration the value of which is significantly less that the value of the consideration provided by the defendent, and

(b) in those circumstances, the preceding provisions of this section shall apply as if the defendant had made a gift of such share in the property as bears to the whole property the same proportion as the difference between the values referred to in paragraph (a) above bears to the value of the consideration provided by the defendant.

Enforcement etc. of confiscation orders

Application of procedure for enforcing fines

6.—(1) Where the Crown Court orders the defendant to pay any amount under section 1 of this Act, section 31(1) to (3C) and 32(1) and (2) of the Powers of Criminal Courts Act 1973 (powers of Crown Court in relation to fines and enforcement of Crown Court fines) shall have effect as if:

(a) that amount were a fine imposed on him by the Crown Court, and

(b) in the Table in section 31 (3A) (imprisonment in default), for the entry relating to an amount exceeding £10,000 there were substituted:

> "An amount exceeding £10,000
> but not exceeding £20,000 .... 12 months
> An amount exceeding £20,000
> but not exceeding £50,000 .... 18 months
> An amount exceeding £50,000
> but not exceeding £100,000 .... 2 years
> An amount exceeding £100,000
> but not exceeding £250,000 .... 3 years
> An amount exceeding £250,000
> but not exceeding £1 millions .... 5 years
> An amount exceeding £1 million .... 10 years".

(2) Where:

(a) a warrant of commitment is issued for default in payment of an amount ordered to be paid under section 1 of this Act in respect of an offence of offences, and

(b) at the time the warrant is issued, the defendant is liable to serve a term of custody in respect of the offence or offences,

118

the term of imprisonment or of detention under section 9 of the Criminal Justice Act 1982 (detention of persons aged 17 to 20 for default) to be served in default of payment of the amount shall not begin to run until after the term mentioned in paragraph *(b)* above.

(3) The reference in subsection (2) above to the term of custody which the defendant is liable to serve in respect of the offence or offences is a reference to the term of imprisonment, youth custody or detention under section 4 or 9 of the said Act of 1982 which he is liable to serve in respect of the offence or offences; and for the purposes of this subsection:

(a) consecutive terms and terms which are wholly or partly concurrent shall be treated as a single term, and

(b) there shall be disregarded:
  (i) any sentence suspended under section 22(1) of the said Act of 1973 which has not taken effect at the time the warrant is issued,
  (ii) in the case of a sentence of imprisonment passed with an order under section 47(1) of the Criminal Law Act 1977, any part of the sentence which the defendant has not at that time been required to serve in prison, and
  (iii) any term of imprisonment or detention fixed under section 31(2) of the said Act of 1973 for which a warrant of commitment has not been issued at that time.

(4) In the application of Part III of the Magistrates' Courts Act 1980 to amounts payable under confiscation orders:

(a) such an amount is not a sum adjudged to be paid by a conviction for the purposes of section 81 (enforcement of fines imposed on young offenders) or a fine for the purposes of section 85 (remission of fines), and

(b) in section 87 (enforcement by High Court or county court), subsection (3) shall be omitted.

(5) The reference in section 143(2) of that Act (power to alter sums specified in certain provisions) to the Table in section 31(3A) of the Powers of Criminal Courts Act 1973 includes a reference to that Table as it has effect by virtue of subsection (1) above.

(6) This section applies in relation to confiscation orders made by the criminal division of the Court of Appeal, or by the House of Lords on appeal from that division, as it applies in relation to confiscation orders made by the Crown Court, and the reference in subsection (1)*(a)* above to the Crown Court shall be construed accordingly.

Cases in which restraint order and charging orders may be made

7.—(1) The powers conferred on the High Court by sections 8(1) and 9(1) of this Act are exercisable where:

(a) proceedings have been instituted in England and Wales against the defendant for a drug trafficking offence,

(b) the proceedings have not been concluded, and

(c) the court is satisfied that there is reasonable cause to believe that the defendant has benefited from drug trafficking.

(2) Those powers are also exercisable where the court is satisfied:

119

(a) that an information is to be laid under section 1 of the Magistrates' Courts Act 1980 that a person has or is suspected of having committed a drug trafficking offence, and

(b) that there is reasonable cause to believe that he has benefited from drug trafficking.

(3) For the purpose of sections 8, 9 and 22 of this Act, at any time when those powers are exercisable before proceedings have been instituted:

(a) references in this Act to the defendant shall be construed as references to the person referred to in subsection (2)(a) above,

(b) references in this Act to the prosecutor shall be construed as references to the person who the High Court is satisfied is to have the conduct of the proposed proceedings, and

(c) references in this Act to realisable property shall be construed as if, immediately before that time, proceedings had been instituted against the person referred to in subsection (2)(a) above for a drug trafficking offence.

(4) Where the court has made an order under section 8(1) or 9(1) of this Act by virtue of subsection (2) above, the court shall discharge the order if the proposed proceedings are not instituted within such time as the court considers reasonable.

Restraint orders

8.—(1) The High Court may by order (in this Act referred to as a "restraint order") prohibit any person from dealing with any realisable property, subject to such conditions and exceptions as may be specified in the order.

(2) A restraint order may apply:

(a) to all realisable property held by a specified person, whether the property is described in the order or not, and

(b) to realisable property held by a specified person, being property transferred to him after the making of the order.

(3) This section shall not have effect in relation to any property for the time being subject to a charge under section 9 of this Act.

(4) A restraint order:

(a) may be made only on an application by the prosecutor,

(b) may be made on an ex parte application to a judge in chambers, and

(c) shall provide for notice to be given to persons affected by the order.

(5) A restraint order:

(a) may be discharged or varied in relation to any property, and

(b) shall be discharged when proceedings for the offences are concluded.

(6) Where the High Court has made a restraint order, the court may at any time appoint a receiver:

(a) to take possession of any realisable property, and

(b) in accordance with the court's directions, to manage or otherwise deal with any property in respect of which he is appointed,

subject to such exceptions and conditions as may be specified by the court; and may require any person having possession of property in respect of which a receiver is appointed under this section to give possession of it to the receiver.

(7) For the purposes of this section, dealing with property held by any person includes (without prejudice to the generality of the expression):

(a) where a debt is owed to that person, making a payment to any person in reduction of the amount of the debt, and

(b) removing the property from Great Britain.

(8) Where the High Court has made a restraint order, a constable may for the purpose of preventing any realisable property being removed from Great Britain, seize the property.

(9) Property seized under subsection (8) above shall be dealt with in accordance with the court's directions.

Charging orders in respect of land, securities etc.

9.—(1) The High Court may make a charging order on realisable property for securing the payment to the Crown:

(a) where a confiscation order has not been made, of an amount equal to the value from time to time of the property charged, and

(b) in any other case, of an amount not exceeding the amount payable under the confiscation order.

(2) For the purposes of this Act, a charging order is an order made under this section imposing on any such realisable property as may be specified in the order a charge for securing the payment of money to the Crown.

(3) A charging order:

(a) may be made only on an application by the prosecutor, and

(b) may be made on an ex parte application to a judge in chambers.

(4) Subject to subsection (6) below, a charge may be imposed by a charging order only on:

(a) any interest in realisable property, being an interest held beneficially by the defendant or by a person to whom the defendant has directly or indirectly made a gift caught by this Act:
   (i)   in any asset of a kind mentioned in subsection (5) below, or
   (ii) under any trust, or

(b) any interest in realisable property held by a person as trustee of a trust if the interest is in such an asset or is an interest under another trust and a charge may by virtue of paragraph *(a)* above be imposed by a charging order on the whole beneficial interest under the first-mentioned trust.

(5) The assets referred to in subsection (4) above are:

(a) land in England and Wales, or

(b) Securities of any of the following kinds:
   (i)   government stock,
   (ii) stock of any body (other than a building society) incorporated within England and Wales,
   (iii) stock of any body incorporated outside England and Wales or of any country or territory outside the United Kingdom, being stock registered in a register kept at any place within England and Wales,
   (iv) units of any unit trust in respect of which a register of the unit holders is kept at any place within England and Wales.

121

(6) In any case where a charge is imposed by a charging order on any interest in an asset of a kind mentioned in subsection (5)*(b)* above, the court may provide for the charge to extend to any interest or dividend payable in respect of the asset.

(7) The court may make an order discharging or varying the charging order and shall make an order discharging the charging order if the proceedings for the offence are concluded or the amount payment of which is secured by the charge is paid into court.

Charging orders: supplemental provisions

10.—(1) A charging order may be made either absolutely or subject to conditions as to notifying any person holding any interest in the property to which the order relates or as to the time when the charge is to become enforceable, or as to other matters.

(2) The Land Charges Act 1972 and the Land Registration Act 1925 shall apply in relation to charging orders as they apply in relation to orders or writs issued or made for the purpose of enforcing judgments.

(3) Where a charging order has been registered under section 6 of the Land Charges Act 1972, subsection (4) of that section (effect of non-registration of writs and orders registrable under that section) shall not apply to an order appointing a receiver made in pursuance of the charging order.

(4) Subject to any provision made under section 11 of this Act or by rules of court, a charge imposed by a charging order shall have the like effect and shall be enforceable in the same courts and in the same manner as an equitable charge created by the person holding the beneficial interest or, as the case may be, the trustees by writing under their hand.

(5) Where a charging order has been protected by an entry registered under the Land Charges Act 1972 or the Land Registration Act 1925, an order under section 9(7) of this Act discharging the charging order may direct that the entry be cancelled.

(6) The Secretary of State may by order made by statutory instrument amend section 9 of this Act by adding to or removing from the kinds of asset for the time being referred to there any asset of a kind which in his opinion ought to be so added or removed.

An order under this subsection shall be subject to annulment in pursuance of a resolution of either House of Parliament.

(7) In this section and section 9 of this Act, "building society", "dividend", "government stock", "stock" and "unit trust" have the same meanings as in the Charging Orders Act 1979.

Realisation of property.

11.—(1) Where:

(a) in proceedings instituted for a drug trafficking offence, a confiscation order is made,

(b) the order is not subject to appeal, and

(c) the proceedings have not been concluded,

the High Court may, on an application by the prosecutor, exercise the powers conferred by subsections (2) to (6) below.

(2) The court may appoint a receiver in respect of realisable property.

(3) The court may empower a receiver appointed under subsection (2) above, under section 8 of this Act or in pursuance of a charging order:

(a) to enforce any charge imposed under section 9 of this Act on realisable property or on interest or dividends payable in respect of such property, and

(b) in relation to any realisable property other than property for the time being subject to a charge under section 9 of this Act, to take possession of the property subject to such conditions or exceptions as may be specified by the court.

(4) The court may order any person having possession of realisable property to give possession of it to any such receiver.

(5) The court may empower any such receiver to realise any realisable property in such manner as the court may direct.

(6) The court may order any person holding an interest in realisable property to make such payment to the receiver in respect of any beneficial interest held by the defendant or, as the case may be, the recipient of a gift caught by this Act as the court may direct and the court may, on the payment being made, by order transfer, grant or extinguish any interest in the property.

(7) Subsection (4) to (6) above do not apply to property for the time being subject to a charge under section 9 of this Act.

(8) The court shall not in respect of any property exercise the powers conferred by subsection (3)(a), (5) or (6) above unless a reasonable opportunity has been given for persons holding any interest in the property to make representations to the court.

Application of proceeds of realisation and other sums.

12.—(1) Subject to subsection (2) below, the following sums in the hands of a receiver appointed under section 8 to 11 of this Act or in pursuance of a charging order, that is:

(a) the proceeds of the enforcement of any charge imposed under section 9 of this Act,

(b) the proceeds of the realisation, other than by the enforcement of such a charge, of any property under section 8 or 11 of this Act, and

(c) any other sums, being property held by the defendant,

shall, after such payments (if any) as the High Court may direct have been made out of those sums, be applied on the defendant's behalf towards the satisfaction of the confiscation order.

(2) If, after the amount payable under the confiscation order has been fully paid, any such sums remain in the hands of such a receiver, the receiver shall distribute those sums:

(a) among such of those who held property which has been realised under this Act, and

(b) in such proportions,

as the High Court may direct after giving a reasonable opportunity for such persons to make representations to the court.

(3) The receipt of any sum by the justices' clerk on account of an amount payable under a confiscation order shall reduce the amount so payable, but the sum shall be applied as follows:

(a) if paid by a receiver under subsection (1) above, it shall first be applied in payment of his remuneration and expenses,

(b) subject to paragraph *(a)* above, it shall be applied in reimbursement of any sums paid by the prosecutor under section 18(2) of this Act,

and the balance shall be treated for the purposes of section 61 of the Justices of the Peace Act 1979 (application for fines, etc.) as if it were a fine imposed by a magistrates' court.

In this subsection, "justices' clerk" has the same meaning as in the Justices of the Peace Act 1979.

Exercise of powers by High Court receiver.

13.—(1) The following provisions apply to the powers conferred on the High Court by sections 8 to 12 of this Act, or on the Court of Session by sections 20 to 22 of this Act, or on a receiver appointed under section 8 or 11 of this Act or in pursuance of a charging order.

(2) Subject to the following provisions of this section, the powers shall be exercised with a view to making available for satisfying the confiscation order or, as the case may be, any confiscation order that may be made in the defendant's case the value for the time being of realisable property held by any person by the realisation of such property.

(3) In the case of realisable property held by a person to whom the defendant has directly or indirectly made a gift caught by this Act, the powers shall be exercised with a view to realising no more than the value for the time being of the gift.

(4) The powers shall be exercised with a view to allowing any person other than the defendant or the recipient of any such gift to retain or recover the value of any property held by him.

(5) An order may be made or other action taken in respect of a debt owed by the Crown.

(6) In exercising those powers, no account shall be taken of any obligations of the defendant or of the recipient of any such gift which conflict with the obligation to satisfy the confiscation order.

Variation of confiscation orders.

14.—(1) If, on an application by the defendent in respect of a confiscation order, the High Court is satisfied that the realisable property is inadequate for the payment of any amount remaining to be recovered under the order the court shall issue a certificate to that effect, giving the court's reasons.

(2) For the purposes of subsection (1) above:

(a) in the case of realisable property held by a person who has been adjudged bankrupt or whose estate has been sequestrated the court shall take into account the extent to which any property held by him may be distributed among creditors, and

(b) the court may disregard any inadequacy in the realisable property which appears to the court to be attributable wholly or partly to anything done by the defendant for the purpose of preserving any property held by a person to whom the defendant had directly or indirectly made a gift caught by this Act from any risk or realisation under this Act.

124

(3) Where a certificate has been issued under subsection (1) above, the defendant may apply to the Crown Court for the amount to be recovered under the order to be reduced.

(4) The Crown Court shall, on an application under subsection (3) above:

(a) substitute for the amount to be recovered under the order such lesser amount as the court thinks just in all the circumstances of the case, and

(b) substitute for the term of imprisonment or of detention fixed under subsection (2) of section 31 of the Powers of Criminal Courts Act 1973 in respect of the amount to be recovered under the order a shorter term determined in accordance with that section (as it has effect by virtue of section 6 of this Act) in respect of the lesser amount.

Bankruptcy of defendant etc.

15.—(1) Where a person who holds realisable property is adjudged bankrupt:

(a) property for the time being subject to a restraint order made before the order adjudging him bankrupt, and

(b) any proceeds of property realised by virtue of section 8(6) or 11(5) or (6) of this Act for the time being in the hands of a receiver appointed under section 8 or 11 of this Act,

is excluded from the bankrupt's estate for the purposes of Part IX of the Insolvency Act 1986.

(2) Where a person has been adjudged bankrupt, the powers conferred on the High Court by sections 8 to 12 of this Act or on a receiver so appointed or on the Court of Session by sections 20 to 22 of this Act shall not be exercised in relation to:

(a) property for the time being comprised in the bankrupt's estate for the purposes of that Part,

(b) property in respect of which his trustee in bankruptcy may (without leave of court) serve a notice under section 307 or 308 of that Act (after-acquired property and tools, clothes etc. exceeding value of reasonable replacement), and

(c) property which is to be applied for the benefit of creditors of the bankrupt by virtue of a condition imposed under section 280(2)(c) of that Act.

(3) Nothing in that Act shall be taken as restricting, or enabling the restriction of, the exercise of those powers.

(4) Subsection (2) above does not affect the enforcement of a charging order:

(a) made before the order adjudging the person bankrupt, or

(b) on property which was subject to a restraint order when the order adjudging him bankrupt was made.

(5) Where, in the case of a debtor, an interim receiver stands appointed under section 286 of that Act and any property of the debtor is subject to a restraint order:

(a) the powers conferred on the receiver by virtue of that Act do not apply to property for the time being subject to the restraint order,

(b) section 287(4) of that Act (receiver's immunity), as it applies to the receiver by virtue of section 286(3) of that Act, shall have effect in relation

125

to such property as if references to such property were substituted for references to property which is not comprised in the bankrupt's estate, and

(c) any such property in the hands of the receiver shall, subject to a lien for any expenses (including his remuneration) properly incurred in respect of the property, be dealt with in such manner as the High Court may direct.

(6) Where a person is adjudged bankrupt and has directly or indirectly made a gift caught by this Act:

(a) no order shall be made under section 339 or 423 of that Act (avoidance of certain transactions) in respect of the making of the gift at any time when proceedings for a drug trafficking offence have been instituted against him and have not been concluded or when property of the person to whom the gift was made is subject to a restraint order or charging order, and

(b) any order made under either of those sections after the conclusion of the proceedings shall take into account any realisation under this Act of property held by the person to whom the gift was made.

(7) In any case in which a petition in bankruptcy is presented, or a receiving order or adjudication in bankruptcy is made, before the date on which the Insolvency Act 1986 comes into force this section has effect with the following modifications:

(a) for references to the bankrupt's estate for the purposes of Part IX of that Act there are substituted references to the property of the bankrupt for the purposes of the Bankruptcy Act 1914,

(b) for references to the Act of 1986 and sections 280(2)(c), 286, 339 and 423 of that Act there are respectively substituted references to the Act of 1914 and to sections 26(2), 8, 27 and 42 of that Act,

(c) the references in subsection (5) to an interim receiver appointed as there mentioned include, where a receiving order has been made, a reference to the receiver constituted by virtue of section 7 of the Act of 1914, and

(d) subsections (2)(b) and (5)(a) and (b) are omitted.

Sequestration in Scotland of defendant etc.

16.—(1) Where the estate of a person who holds realisable property is sequestrated:

(a) property for the time being subject to a restraint order made before the award of sequestration, and

(b) any proceeds of property realised by virtue of section 8(6) or 11(5) or (6) of this Act for the time being in the hands of a receiver appointed under section 8 or 11 of this Act,

is excluded from the debtor's estate for the purposes of the Bankruptcy (Scotland) Act 1985.

(2) Where an award of sequestration has been made, the powers conferred on the High Court by sections 8 to 12 of this Act or on a receiver so appointed or on the Court of Session by sections 20 to 22 of this Act shall not be exercised in relation to:

(a) property comprised in the whole estate of the debtor within the meaning of section 31(8) of that Act,

126

(b) any income of the debtor which has been ordered, under subsection (2) of section 32 of that Act, to be paid to the permanent trustee or any estate which, under subsection (6) of that section, vests in the permanent trustee.

(3) Nothing in that Act shall be taken as restricting, or enabling the restriction of, the exercise of those powers.

(4) Subsection (2) above does not affect the enforcement of a charging order:

(a) made before the award of sequestration, or
(b) on property which was subject to a restraint order when the award of sequestration was made.

(5) Where, during the period before sequestration is awarded, an interim trustee stands appointed under the proviso to section 13(1) of that Act and any property in the debtor's estate is subject to a restraint order:

(a) the powers conferred on the trustee by virtue of that Act do not apply to property for the time being subject to the restraint order,
(b) the trustee if he seizes or disposes of any property for the time being subject to the restraint order and, when he does so, believes and has reasonable grounds for believing that he is entitled (whether in pursuance of an order of a court or otherwise) to do so:
  (i) shall not (except insofar as the same has been caused by his negligence) be liable to any person in respect of any loss or damage resulting from his seizure or disposal of the property, and
  (ii) shall have a lien on the property, or the proceeds of its sale, for such of the expenses of the sequestrations as were incurred in connection with the seizure or disposal, and
(c) any such property in the hands of the trustee shall, subject to a lien for any expenses (including his remuneration) properly incurred in respect of the property, be dealt with in such manner as the High Court may direct.

(6) Where the estate of a person is sequestrated and he has directly or indirectly made a gift caught by this Act:

(a) no decree shall be granted under section 34 or 36 of that Act (gratuitous alienations and unfair preferences) in respect of the making of the gift at any time when proceedings for a drug trafficking offence have been instituted against him and have not been concluded or when property of the person to whom the gift was made is subject to a restraint order or charging order, and
(b) any decree made under either of those sections after the conclusion of the proceedings shall take into account any realisation under this Act of property held by the person to whom the gift was made.

(7) In any case in which, notwithstanding the coming into force of the Bankruptcy (Scotland) Act 1985 the Bankruptcy (Scotland) Act 1913 applies to a sequestration, subsection (2) above shall have effect as if for paragraphs *(a)* and *(b)* thereof there were substituted the following paragraphs:

"*(a)* property compromised in the whole property of the debtor which vests in the trustee under section 97 of the Bankruptcy (Scotland) Act 1913,

(b) any income of the bankrupt which has been ordered under subsection (2) of section 98 of that Act, to be paid to the trustee or any estate which, under subsection (1) of that section, vests in the trustee";

and subsection (3) above shall have effect as if for the reference therein to the Act of 1985 there were substituted a reference to the Act of 1913.

Winding up of company holding realisable property

17.—(1) Where realisable property is held by a company and an order for the winding up of the company has been made or a resolution has been passed by the company for the voluntary winding up, the functions of the liquidator (or any provisional liquidator) shall not be exercisable in relation to:

(a) property for the time being subject to a restraint order made before the relevant time, and

(b) any proceeds of property realised by virtue of section 8(6) or 11(5) or (6) of this Act for the time being in the hands of a receiver appointed under section 8 or 11 of this Act;

but there shall be payable out of such property any expenses (including the remuneration of the liquidator or provisional liquidator) properly incurred in the winding up in respect of the property.

(2) Where, in the case of a company, such an order has been made or such a resolution has been passed, the powers conferred on the High Court by sections 8 to 12 of this Act or on a receiver so appointed or in the Court of Session by sections 20 to 22 of this Act shall not be exercised in relation to any realisable property held by the company in relation to which the functions of the liquidator are exercisable:

(a) so as to inhibit him from exercising those functions for the purpose of distributing any property held by the company to the company's creditors, or

(b) so as to prevent the payment out of any property of expenses (including the remuneration of the liquidator or any provisional liquidator) properly incurred in the winding up in respect of the property.

(3) Nothing in the Insolvency Act 1986 shall be taken as restricting, or enabling the restriction of, the exercise of those powers.

(4) Subsection (2) above does not affect the enforcement of a charging order made before the relevant time or on property which was subject to restraint order at the relevant time.

(5) In this section:

"company" means any company which may be wound up under the Insolvency Act 1986; and

"the relevant time" means:

(a) where no order for the winding up of the company has been made, the time of the passing of the resolution for voluntary winding up,

(b) where such an order has been made and, before the presentation of the petition for the winding up of the company by the court, such a resolution had been passed by the company, the time of the passing of the resolution, and

(c) in any other case where such an order has been made, the time of the making of the order.

(6) In any case in which a winding up of a company has commenced, or is treated as having commenced, before the date on which the Insolvency Act 1986 comes into force, this section has effect with the substitution for references to that Act of references to the Companies Act 1985.

Receivers: supplementary provisions

18.—(1) Where a receiver appointed under section 8 or 11 of this Act or in pursuance of a charging order takes any action:

(a) in relation to property which is not realisable property, being action which he would be entitled to take if it were such property,
(b) believing, and having reasonable grounds for believing, that he is entitled to take that action in relation to that property,

he shall not be liable to any person in respect of any loss or damage resulting from his action except in so far as the loss or damage is caused by his negligence.

(2) Any amount due in respect of the remuneration and expenses of a receiver so appointed shall, if no sum is available to be applied in payment of it under section 12(3)(a) of this Act, be paid by the prosecutor or, in a case where proceedings for a drug trafficking offence are not instituted, by the person on whose application the receiver was appointed.

Compensation

19.—(1) If proceedings are instituted against a person for a drug trafficking offence or offences and either:

(a) the proceedings do not result in his conviction for any drug trafficking offence, or
(b) where he is convicted of one or more drug trafficking offences:
　　(i) the conviction or convictions concerned are quashed (and no conviction for any drug trafficking offence is substituted), or
　　(ii) he is pardoned by Her Majesty in respect of the conviction or convictions concerned,

the High Court may, on an application by a person who held property which was realisable property, order compensation to be paid to the applicant.

(2) The High Court shall not order compensation to be paid in any case unless the court is satisfied:

(a) that there has been some serious default on the part of a person concerned in the investigation or prosecution of the offence or offences concerned, being a person mentioned in subsection (4) below, and that, but for that default, the proceedings would not have been instituted or continued, and
(b) that the applicant has suffered substantial loss in consequence of anything done in relation to the property by or in pursuance of
　　(i) an order of the High Court under sections 8 to 11 of this Act, or
　　(ii) an order of the Court of Session under section 20, 21 or 22 of this Act.

129

(3) The amount of compensation to be paid under this section shall be such as the High Court thinks just in all the circumstances of the case.

(4) Compensation payable under this section shall be paid:

(a) where the person in default was or was acting as a member of a police force, out of the police fund out of which the expenses of that police force are met,

(b) where the person in default was a member of the Crown Prosecution Service or acting on behalf of the service, by the Director of Public Prosecutions, and

(c) where the person in default was an officer within the meaning of the Customs and Excise Management Act 1979, by the Commissioners of Customs and Excise.

Enforcement in Scotland

Recognition and enforcement in Scotland of orders and functions under sections 8, 11, 12 and 30.

20.—(1) An order to which this section applies shall, subject to this section and section 21 of this Act, have effect in the law of Scotland but shall be enforced in Scotland only in accordance with this section and that section.

(2) A receiver's functions under or for the purposes of section 8, 11 or 12 of this Act shall, subject to this section and section 21 of this Act, have effect in the law of Scotland.

(3) If an order to which this section applies is registered under this section:

(a) the Court of Session shall have, in relation to its enforcement, the same power,

(b) proceedings for or with respect to its enforcement may be taken, and

(c) proceedings for or with respect to any contravention of such an order (whether before or after such registration) may be taken,

as if the order had originally been made in that Court.

(4) Nothing in this section enables any provision of an order which empowers a receiver to do anything in Scotland under section 11(3)(a) of this Act to have effect in the law of Scotland.

(5) The orders to which this section applies are orders of the High Court:

(a) made under sections 8, 11, 12 or 30 of this Act,

(b) relating to the exercise by that Court of its powers under those sections, or

(c) relating to receivers in the performance of their functions under sections 8, 11 or 12 of this Act,

but not including an order in proceedings for enforcement of any such order.

(6) References in this section to an order under section 8 of this Act include references to a discharge under section 7(4) of this Act of such an order.

(7) In this section and in sections 21 and 23, "order" means any order, direction or judgment (by whatever name called).

(8) Nothing in any order of the High Court under section 11(6) of this Act prejudices any enactment or rule of law in respect of the recording of deeds relating to heritable property in Scotland or the registration of interests therein.

Provisions supplementary to section 20.

21.—(1) The Court of Session shall, on application made to it in accordance with rules of court for registration of an order to which section 20 applies, direct that the order shall, in accordance with such rules, be registered in that Court.

(2) Subsections (1) and (3) of section 20 of this Act and subsection (1) above are subject to any provision made by rules of court:

(a) as to the manner in which and conditions subject to which orders to which that section applies are to be enforced in Scotland,

(b) For the sisting of proceedings for enforcement of such an order,

(c) for the modification or cancellation of the registration of such an order if the order is modified or revoked or ceases to have effect.

(3) This section and section 20 are without prejudice to any enactment or rule of law as to the effect of notice or the want of it in relation to orders of the High Court.

(4) The Court of Session shall have the like power to make an order under section 1 of the Administration of Justice (Scotland) Act 1972 (extended power to order inspection of documents etc.) in relation to proceedings brought or likely to be brought under this Act in the High Court as if those proceedings had been brought or were likely to be brought in the Court of Session.

(5) The Court of Session may, additionally, for the purpose of:

(a) assisting the achievement in Scotland of the purposes of orders to which section 20 of this Act applies, or

(b) assisting receivers performing functions there under or for the purposes of section 8, 11 or 12 of this Act,

make such orders and do otherwise as seems to it appropriate.

Inhibition and arrestment of property in Scotland.

22.—(1) On the application of the prosecutor, the Court of Session may, in repect of any property in Scotland, being property to which a restraint order registered in that Court relates:

(a) where the property is heritable, grant warrant for inhibition in respect of the property against any person with an interest in it, or

(b) where the property is moveable and would, if the person entitled to it were a debtor, be arrestable property, grant warrant for arrestment of the property,

and on the grant of such a warrant the enactments and rules of law relating to inhibition and arrestment shall, subject to the provisions of this section, apply respectively as if the warrant had been granted on the dependence of an action for debt at the instance of the prosecutor against the person against whom the warrant for inhibition is granted or, as the case may be, whose property falls to be arrested.

(2) Section 155 of the Titles to Land Consolidation (Scotland) Act 1868 (effective data of inhibitions) shall apply in relation to an inhibition proceedings upon a warrant under this section.

(3) In the application of section 158 of the said Act of 1868 (recall of inhibitions) to an inhibition proceeding upon a warrant under this section, the

references to a particular Lord Ordinary in the Court of Session shall be construed as references to any such Lord Ordinary.

(4) Any power of the Court of Session to recall, loose or restrict inhibitions or arrestments shall, in relation to an inhibition or arrestment proceeding upon a warrant under this section and without prejudice to any other consideration lawfully applying to the exercise of the power, be eercised with a view to achieving the purposes specified in section 13 of this Act.

(5) The Court of Session shall have power to restrict the effect of an inhibition proceeding upon a warrant under this section to particular property.

(6) The fact that such an inhibition or arrestment has been executed as respects any property shall not prejudice the exercise of a receiver's powers under or for the purposes of section 8, 11 or 12 of this Act in respect of that property.

(7) An inhibition or arrestment under this section shall cease to have effect upon the restraint order to which it relates ceasing to have effect and, where an inhibition ceases to have effect, it shall thereupon be the duty of the prosecutor to discharge it.

Proof in Scotland of High Court Orders

23. A document purporting to be a copy of an order under or for the purposes of this Act by the High Court and to be certified as such by a proper officer of that Court shall, in Scotland, be sufficient evidence of the order.

Offence of assisting drug traffickers

Assisting another to retain the benefit of drug trafficking

24.—(1) Subject to subsection (3) below, if a person enters into or is otherwise concerned in an arrangement whereby:

(a) the retention or control by or on behalf of another (call him "A") of A's proceeds of drug trafficking is facilitated (whether by concealment, removal from the jurisdiction, transfer to nominees or otherwise), or
(b) A's proceeds of drug trafficking:
    (i) are used to secure that funds are placed at A's disposal, or
    (ii) are used for A's benefit to acquire property by way of investment,

knowing or suspecting that A is a person who carries on or has carried on drug trafficking or has benefited from drug trafficking, he is guilty of an offence.

(2) In this section, references to any person's proceeds of drug trafficking include a reference to any property which in whole or in part directly or indirectly represented in his hands his proceeds of drug trafficking.

(3) Where a person discloses to a constable a suspicion or belief that any funds or investments are derived from or used in connection with drug trafficking or any matter on which such a suspicion or belief is based:

(a) the disclosure shall not be treated as a breach of any restriction upon disclosure of information imposed by contract, and
(b) if he does any act in contravention of subsection (1) above and the disclosure relates to the arrangement concerned, he does not commit an offence under this section if the disclosure is made in accordance with this paragraph, that is:

(i) it is made before he does the act concerned being an act done with the consent of the constable, or

(ii) it is made after he does the act, but is made on his initiative and as soon as it is reasonable for him to make it.

(4) In proceedings against a person for an offence under this section, it is a defence to prove:

(a) that he did not know or suspect that the arrangement related to any person's proceeds of drug trafficking, or

(b) that he did not know or suspect that by the arrangement the retention or control by or on behalf of A of any property was facilitated or, as the case may be, that by the arrangement any property was used as mentioned in subsection (1) above, or

(c) that:

(i) he intended to disclose to a constable such a suspicion, belief or matter as is mentioned in subsection (3) above in relation to the arrangement, but

(ii) there is reasonable excuse for his failure to make disclosure in accordance with subsection (3)*(b)* above.

(5) A person guilty of an offence under this section shall be liable:

(a) on conviction on indictment, to imprisonment for a term not exceeding fourteen years or to a fine or to both, and

(b) on summary conviction, to imprisonment for a term not exceeding six months or to a fine not exceeding the statutory maximum or to both.

(6) In Part II of Schedule 1 to the Criminal Justice Act 1982 (persons convicted of offences under certain enactments not eligible for early release), after paragraph 25 there is inserted:

"DRUG TRAFFICKING OFFENCES ACT 1986 (c. 32)
26. Section 24 (assisting another to retain the benefit of drug trafficking)."

Enforcement of external orders

Enforcement of Northern Ireland orders

25.—(1) Her Majesty may by Order in Council provide that, for the purposes of sections 7 to 19 of this Act, this Act shall have effect as if:

(a) references to confiscation orders included a reference to orders made by courts in Northern Ireland which appear to Her Majesty to correspond to confiscation orders,

(b) references to drug trafficking offences included a reference to any offence under the law of Northern Ireland (not being a drug trafficking offence) which appears to Her Majesty to correspond to such an offence,

(c) references to proceedings in England and Wales or to the institution or conclusion in England and Wales of proceedings included a reference to proceedings in Northern Ireland or to the institution or conclusion in Northern Ireland of proceedings, as the case may be, and

(d) references to the laying of an information or the issue of a summons or warrant under section 1 of the Magistrates' Courts Act 1980 included a

133

reference to making a complaint or issuing a summons or warrant (as the case may be) under Article 20 of the Magistrates' Courts (Northern Ireland) Order 1981.

(2) An Order in Council under this section may provide for those sections to have effect in relation to anything done or to be done in Northern Ireland subject to such further modifications as may be specified in the order.

(3) An Order in Council varying or revoking a previous Order in Council under this section may contain such incidental, consequential and transitional provisions as Her Majesty considers expedient.

(4) An Order in Council under this section shall not be made unless a draft of the order has been laid before Parliament and approved by resolution of each House of Parliament.

Enforcement of other external orders

26.—(1) Her Majesty may by Order in Council apply this section to any order made after the Order in Council comes into force by a court of a country or territory outside the United Kingdom, being an Order:

(a) of a description specified in the Order in Council, and

(b) made for the purpose of recovering payments or other rewards received in connection with drug trafficking or their value.

(2) An order to which this section applies is referred to below in this section as an "external confiscation order"; and in this section "designated country" means a country or territory outside the United Kingdom designated by an Order in Council under this section.

(3) The High Court may, on an application by or on behalf of the government of a designated country, register an external confiscation order made there, subject to subsection (4) below.

(4) The High Court shall not register an external confiscation order unless:

(a) the court is satisfied that at the time of registration the order is in force in the designated country and is not subject to appeal in the designated country,

(b) the court is satisfied, where the person against whom the order is made did not appear in the proceedings, that he received notice of the proceedings in sufficient time to enable him to defend them, and

(c) the court is of the opinion that enforcing the order in England and Wales would not be contrary to the interests of justice.

(5) The High Court shall cancel the registration of an external confiscation order if it appears to the court that the order has been satisfied (whether by payment of the amount due under the order, by the person against whom the order is made serving imprisonment in default or otherwise).

(6) In relation to an external confiscation order registered under this section, sections 8 to 18 of this Act shall have effect subject to such modifications as may be specified in an Order in Council under this section as they have effect in relation to a confiscation order.

(7) In subsection (4) above, "appeal" includes any proceedings by way of discharging or setting aside a judgment or an application for a new trial or a stay of execution.

134

(8) In any case where the High Court is satisfied, on an application by or on behalf of the government of a designated country, that proceedings which might result in an external confiscation order being made against a person have been instituted in the designated country and have not been concluded, sections 8 to 10 of this Act shall have effect in relation to those proceedings:

(a) as they would have effect in relation to proceedings instituted in England and Wales against that person for a drug trafficking offence which have not been concluded, and

(b) as if references to a confiscation order were references to an external confiscation order and references to an application by the prosecutor were references to an application by or on behalf of that government, and

(c) subject to such other modifications as may be specified in an Order in Council under this section.

(9) An Order in Council under this section may include such provision:

(a) as to evidence or proof of any matter for the purposes of this section, and

(b) as to the circumstances in which proceedings are to be treated for those purposes as instituted or concluded in any designated country.

as Her Majesty considers expedient.

(10) An Order in Council varying or revoking a previous Order in Council under this section may contain such incidental, consequential and transitional provisions as Her Majesty considers expedient.

(11) An Order in Council under this section shall not be made unless a draft of the order has been laid before Parliament and approved by resolution of each House of Parliament.

Investigations into drug trafficking

Order to make material available

27.—(1) A constable or, in Scotland, the procurator fiscal may, for the purpose of an investigation into drug trafficking apply to a Circuit judge or, in Scotland, the sheriff for an order under subsection (2) below in relation to particular material or material of a particular description.

(2) If on such an application the judge or, as the case may be, the sheriff is satisfied that the conditions in subsection (4) below are fulfilled, he may make an order that the person who appears to him to be in possession of the material to which the application relates shall:

(a) produce it to a constable for him to take away, or

(b) give a constable access to it,

within such period as the order may specify.

This subsection is subject to section 30(11) of this Act.

(3) The period to be specified in an order under subsection (2) above shall be seven days unless it appears to the judge or, as the case may be, the sheriff that a longer or shorter period would be appropriate in the particular circumstances of the application.

(4) The conditions referred to in subsection (2) above are:

(a) that there are reasonable grounds for suspecting that a specified person has carried on or has benefited from drug trafficking,

135

(b) that there are reasonable grounds for suspecting that the material to which the application relates:
  - (i) is likely to be of substantial value (whether by itself or together with other material) to the investigation for the purpose of which the application is made, and
  - (ii) does not consist of or include items subject to legal privilege or excluded material, and

  (c) that there are reasonable grounds for believing that it is in the public interest, having regard:
  - (i) to the benefit likely to accrue to the investigation if the material is obtained, and
  - (ii) to the circumstances under which the person in possession of the material holds it,

  that the material should be produced or that access to it should be given.

(5) Where the judge or, as the case may be, the sheriff makes an order under subsection (2)(*b*) above in relation to material on any premises he may, on the application of a constable or, in Scotland, the procurator fiscal order any person who appears to him to be entitled to grant entry to the premises to allow a constable to enter the premises to obtain access to the material.

(6) Provision may be made by Crown Court Rules or, as respects Scotland, rules of court as to:

(a) the discharge and variation of order under this section, and

(b) proceedings relating to such orders.

(7) An order of a Circuit Judge under this section shall have effect as if it were an order of the Crown Court.

(8) Where the material to which an application under this section relates consists of information contained in a computer:

(a) an order under subsection (2)*(a)* above shall have effect as an order to produce the material in a form in which it can be taken away and in which it is visible and legible, and

(b) an order under subsection (2)*(b)* above shall have effect as an order to give access to the material in a form in which it is visible and legible.

(9) An order under subsection (2) above:

(a) shall not confer any right to production of, or access to, items subject to legal privilege or excluded material,

(b) shall have effect notwithstanding any obligation as to secrecy or other restriction upon the disclosure of information imposed by statute or otherwise, and

(c) may be made in relation to material in the possession of an authorised government department.

Authority for search

28.—(1) A constable or, in Scotland, the procurator fiscal may, for the purpose of an investigation into drug trafficking, apply to a Circuit judge or, in Scotland, the sheriff for a warrant under this section in relation to specified premises.

(2) On such application the judge or, as the case may, the sheriff may issue a warrant authorising a constable to enter and search the premises if he is satisfied:

136

(a) that an order made under section 27 of this Act in relation to material on the premises has not been compiled with, or

(b) that the conditions in subsection (3) below are fulfilled, or

(c) that the conditions in subsection (4) below are fulfilled.

(3) The conditions referred to in subsection (2)*(b)* above are:

(a) that there are reasonable grounds for suspecting that a specified person has carried on or has benefited from drug trafficking, and

(b) that the conditions in section 27(4)*(b)* and *(c)* of this Act are fulfilled in relation to any material on the premises, and

(c) that it would not be appropriate to make an order under that section in relation to the material because:

    (i)   it is not practicable to communicate with any person entitled to produce the material, or

    (ii) it is not practicable to communicate with any person entitled to grant access to the material or entitled to grant entry to the premises on which the material is situated, or

    (iii) the investigation for the purposes of which the application is made might be seriously prejudiced unless a constable could secure immediate access to the material.

(4) The conditions referred to in subsection (2)*(c)* above are:

(a) that there are reasonable grounds for suspecting that a specified person has carried on or has benefited from drug trafficking, and

(b) that there are reasonable grounds for suspecting that there is on the premises material relating to the specified person or to drug trafficking which is likely to be of substantial value (whether by itself or together with other material) to the investigation for the purpose of which the application is made, but that the material cannot at the time of the application be particularised, and

(c) that:

    (i)   it is not practicable to communicate with any person entitled to grant entry to the premises, or

    (ii) entry to the premises will not be granted unless a warrant is produced, or

    (iii) the investigation for the purpose of which the application is made might be seriously prejudiced unless a constable arriving at the premises could secure immediate entry to them.

(5) Where a constable has entered premises in the execution of a warrant issued under this section, he may seize and retain any material, other than items subject to legal privilege and excluded material, which is likely to be of substantial value (whether by itself or together with other material) to the investigation for the purpose of which the warrant was issued.

Sections 27 and 28: supplementary provisions

29.—(1) . . .[1]

(2) Subject to subsection (3) below, in sections 27 and 28 of this Act "items subject to legal privilege", "excluded material" and "premises" have the same meanings as in the said Act of 1984.

1   Reproduced in Appendix IX of this supplement.

(3) As respects Scotland, in sections 27 and 28 of this Act the references to excluded material shall be omitted, and:

"items subject to legal privilege" means:

(a) communications between a professional legal adviser and his client,
(b) communications made in connection with or in contemplation of legal proceedings and for the purposes of these proceedings,

being communications which would in legal proceedings be protected from disclosure by virtue of any rule of law relating to the confidentiality of communications, and

"premises" includes any place and, in particular, includes:

(a) any vehicle, vessel, aircraft or hovercraft,
(b) any offshore intallation within the meaning of section 1 of the Mineral Workings (Offshore Installations) Act 1971, and
(c) any tent or movable structure.

Disclosure of information held by government departments

30.—(1) Subject to subsection (4) below, the High Court may on an application by the prosecutor order any material mentioned in subsection (3) below which is in the possession of an authorised government department to be produced to the court within such period as the court may specify.

(2) The power to make an order under subsection (1) above is exercisable if:

(a) the powers conferred on the court by sections 8(1) and 9(1) of this Act are exercisable by virtue of subsection (1) of section 7 of this Act, or
(b) those powers are exercisable by virtue of subsection (2) of that section and the court has made a restraint or charging order which has not been discharged;

but where the power to make an order under subsection (1) above is exercisable by virtue only of paragraph *(b)* above, subsection (3) of section 7 of this Act shall apply for the purposes of this section as it applies for the purposes of sections 8 and 9 of this Act.

(3) The material referred to in subsection (1) above is any material which:

(a) has been submitted to an officer of an authorised government department by the defendant or by a person who has at any time held property which was realisable property,
(b) has been made by an officer of an authorised government department in relation to the defendant or such a person, or
(c) is correspondence which passed between an officer of an authorised government department and the defendant or such a person,

and an order under that subsection may require the production of all such material or of a particular description of such material, being material in the possession of the department concerned.

(4) An order under subsection (1) above shall not require the production of any material unless it appears to the High Court that the material is likely to contain information that would facilitate the exercise of the powers conferred on the court by sections 8 to 11 of this Act or on a receiver appointed under section 8 or 11 of this Act or in pursuance of a charging order.

(5) The court may by order authorise the disclosure to such a receiver of any material produced under subsection (1) above or any part of such material; but the court shall not make an order under this subsection unless a reasonable opportunity has been given for an officer of the department to make representations to the court.

(6) Material disclosed in pursuance of an order under subsection (5) above may, subject to any conditions contained in the order, be further disclosed for the purposes of the functions under this Act of the receiver or the Crown Court.

(7) The court may by order authorise the disclosure to a person mentioned in subsection (8) below of any material produced under subsection (1) above or any part of such material; but the court shall not make an order under this subsection unless:

(a)   a reasonable opportunity has been given for an officer of the department to make representations to the court, and

(b)   it appears to the court that the material is likely to be of substantial value in exercising functions relating to drug trafficking.

(8) The persons referred to in subsection (7) above are:

(a)   an member of a police force,

(b)   any member of the Crown Prosecution Service, and

(c)   any officer within the meaning of the Customs and Excise Management Act 1979.

(9) Material disclosed in pursuance of an order under subsection (7) above may, subject to any conditions contained in the order, be further disclosed for the purposes of functions relating to drug trafficking.

(10) Material may be produced or disclosed in pursuance of this section notwithstanding any obligation as to secrecy or other restriction upon the disclosure of information imposed by statute or otherwise.

(11) An order under subsection (1) above and, in the case of material in the possession of an authorised government department, an order under section 27(2) of this Act may require any officer of the department (whether named in the order or not) who may for the time being be in possession of the material concerned to comply with it, and such an order shall be served as if the proceedings were civil proceedings against the department.

(12) The person on whom such an order is served:

(a)   shall take all reasonable steps to bring it to the attention of the officer concerned, and

(b)   if the order is not brought to that officer's attention within the period referred to in subsection (1) above, shall report the reasons for the failure to the court;

and it shall also be the duty of any other officer of the department in receipt of the order to take such steps as are mentioned in paragraph (a) above.

Offence of prejudicing investigation

31.—(1) Where, in relation to an investigation into drug trafficking, an order under section 27 of this Act has been made or has been applied for and has not been refused or a warrant under section 28 of this Act has been issued, a person who, knowing or suspecting that the investigation is taking place, makes any disclosure which is likely to prejudice the investigation is guilty of an offence.

(2) In proceedings against a person for an offence under this section, it is a defence to prove:

(*a*) that he did not know or suspect that the disclosure was likely to prejudice the investigation, or

(*b*) that he had lawful authority or reasonable excuse for making the disclosure.

(3) A person guilty of an offence under this section shall be liable:

(*a*) on conviction on indictment, to imprisonment for a term not exceeding five years or to a fine or to both, and

(*b*) on summary conviction, to imprisonment for a term not exceeding six months or to a fine not exceeding the statutory maximum or to both.

32.—. . .[2]

Miscellaneous and Supplemental

Power to inspect Land Register etc.

33.—(1) The Chief Land Registrar (in this section referred to as "the registrar") shall, on an application under subsection (2) or (4) below made in relation to a person specified in the application or to property so specified, provide the applicant with any information kept by the registrar under the Land Registration Act 1925 which relates to the person or property so specified.

(2) An application may be made by:

(*a*) any police officer not below the rank of superintendent,

(*b*) any Crown Prosecutor, or

(*c*) any person commissioned by the Commissioners of Customs and Excise not below the rank of senior executive officer,

and on an application under this subsection an appropriate certificate shall be given to the registrar.

(3) In subsection (2) above, "appropriate certificate" means a certificate:

(*a*) that there are reasonable grounds for suspecting that there is information kept by the registrar which is likely to be of substantial value (whether by itself or together with other information) to an investigation into drug trafficking, or

(*b*) that:

(i) a person specified in the certificate has committed or there are reasonable grounds for suspecting that a person so specified has committed a drug trafficking offence, and

(ii) there are reasonable grounds for suspecting that there is information kept by the registrar which is likely to be of substantial value (whether by itself or together with other information) to an investigation into whether the person so specified has benefited from drug trafficking or in facilitating the recovery of the value of his proceeds of drug trafficking.

---

2 Reproduced in Appendix IX of this supplement.

(4) An application may be made by a receiver appointed under section 8 or 11 of this Act and on an application under this subsection there shall be given to the registrar:

(a) a document certified by the proper officer of the court to be a true copy of the order appointing the receiver, and

(b) a certificate that there are reasonable grounds for suspecting that there is information kept by the registrar which is likely to facilitate the exercise of the powers conferred on the receiver in respect of the person or property specified in the application.

(5) The reference in subsection (1) above to the provision of information is a reference to its provision in documentary form.

34.—. . .[3]

Miscellaneous and Supplemental

Power to appoint additional assistant commissioners

35.—(1) In section 2 of the Metropolitan Police Act 1856 (power to appoint two assistant commissioners of police for the metropolis, increased to five by the Metropolitan Police Act 133) for the word "two" there is substituted "six"; and the Metropolitan Police Act 1933 is repealed.

36.—. . .[4]

Expenses

37. There shall be paid out of money provided by Parliament any increase attributable to this Act in the sums payable out of money so provided under any other Act.

General interpretation

38.—(1) In this Act:

"authorised government department" means a government department which is an authorised department for the purposes of the Crown Proceedings Act 1947;

"constable" includes a person commissioned by the Commissioners of Customs and Excise;

"corresponding law" has the same meaning as in the Misuse of Drugs Act 1971;

"drug trafficking" means doing or being concerned in any of the following, whether in England and Wales or elsewhere:

(a) producing or supplying a controlled drug where the production or supply contravenes section 4(1) of the Misuse of Drugs Act 1971 or a corresponding law;

(b) transporting or storing a controlled drug where possession of the drug contravenes section 5(1) of that Act or a corresponding law;

3 Reproduced in Appendix III to this supplement.
4 Reproduced in Appendix IX to this supplement.

(c)   importing or exporting a controlled drug where the importation or exportation is prohibited by section 3(1) of that Act or a corresponding law;

and includes a person doing the following, whether in England and Wales or elsewhere, that is entering into or being otherwise concerned in an arrangement whereby:
  (i)   the retention or control by or on behalf of another person of the other person's proceeds of drug trafficking is facilitated, or
  (ii) the proceeds of drug trafficking by another person are used to secure that funds are placed at the other person's disposal or are used for the other person's benefit to acquire property by way of investment;

"drug trafficking offence" means any of the following:

(a)   an offence under section 4(2) or (3) or 5(3) or the Misuse of Drugs Act 1971 (production, supply and possession for supply of controlled drugs);
(b)   an offence under section 20 of that Act (assisting in or inducing commission outside United Kingdom of offence punishable under a corresponding law);
(c)   an offence under:
  (i)   section 50(2) or (3) of the Customs and Excise Management Act 1979 (improper importation),
  (ii) section 68(2) of that Act (exportation), or
  (iii) section 170 of that Act (fraudulent evasion),
  in connection with a prohibition or restriction on importation or exportation having effect by virtue of section 3 of the Misuse of Drugs Act 1971;

(d)   an offence under section 24 of this Act;
(e)   an offence under section 1 of the Criminal Law Act 1977 of conspiracy to commit any of the offences in paragraphs (a) to (d) above;
(f)   an offence under section 1 of the Criminal Attempts Act 1981 of attempting to commit any of those offences;
(g)   an offence of inciting another to commit any of those offences, whether under section 19 of the Misuse of Drugs Act 1971 or at common law; and
(h)   aiding, abetting, counselling or procuring the commission of any of those offences;

"interest", in relation to property, includes right;
"property" includes money and all other property, real or personal, heritable or moveable, including things in action and other intangible or incorporeal property.

(2) The expressions listed in the left hand column below are respectively defined or (as the case may be) fall to be construed in accordance with the provisions of this Act listed in the right hand column in relation to those expressions.

Expression	*Relevant provision*
Benefited from drug trafficking	Section 1(3)
Charging order	Section 9(2)
Confiscation order	Section 1(8)

Dealing with property	Section 8(7)
Defendant	Section 1(8)
Gift caught by this Act	Section 5(9)
Making a gift	Section 5(10)
Proceeds of drug trafficking	Section 2(1)(*a*)
Realisable property	Section 5(1)
Restraint order	Section 8(1)
Value of gift, payment or reward	Section 5
Value of proceeds of drug trafficking	Section 2(1)(*b*)
Value of property	Section 5(4).

(3) This Act applies to property whether it is situated in England and Wales or elsewhere.

(4) References in this Act to offences include a reference to offences committed before the commencement of section 1 of this Act; but nothing in this Act imposes any duty or confers any power on any court in or in connection with proceedings against a person for a drug trafficking offence instituted before the commencement of that section.

(5) References in this Act to anything received in connection with drug trafficking include a reference to anything received both in that connection and in some other connection.

(6) The following provisions shall have effect for the interpretation of this Act.

(7) Property is held by any person if he holds any interest in it.

(8) References to property held by a person include a reference to property vested in his trustee in bankruptcy, permanent or interim trustee within the meaning of the Bankruptcy (Scotland) Act 1985 or liquidator.

(9) References to an interest held by a person beneficially in property include a reference to an interest which would be held by him beneficially if the property were not so vested.

(10) Property is transferred by one person to another if the first transfers or grants to the other any interest in the property.

(11) Proceedings for an offence are instituted in England and Wales:

(*a*)   when a justice of the peace issues a summons or warrant under section 1 of the Magistrates' Courts Act 1980 in respect of the offence,

(*b*)   when a person is charged with the offence after being taken into custody without a warrant,

(*c*)   when a bill of indictment is preferred under section 2 of the Administration of Justice (Miscellaneous Provisions) Act 1933 in a case falling within paragraph (*b*) of subsection (2) of that section;

and where the application of this subsection would result in there being more than one time for the institution of proceedings, they shall be taken to have been instituted at the earliest of those times.

(12) Proceedings in England and Wales for an offence are concluded on the occurrence of one of the following events:

(*a*)   the discontinuance of the proceedings;

(*b*)   the acquittal of the defendant;

(*c*)   the quashing of his conviction for the offence;

(*d*)   the grant of Her Majesty's pardon in respect of his conviction for the offence;

(e)   the court sentencing or otherwise dealing with him in respect of his conviction for the offence without having made a confiscation order; and

(f)   the satisfaction of a confiscation order made in the proceedings (whether by payment of the amount due under the order or by the defendant serving imprisonment in default).

(13) An order is subject to appeal so long as an appeal or further appeal is pending against the order or (if it was made on a conviction) against the conviction; and for this purpose an appeal or further appeal shall be treated as pending (where one is competent but has not been brought) until the expiration of the time for bringing that appeal.

Minor amendments

39.—(1) Section 28 of the Bankruptcy Act 1914 (effect of order of discharge) shall have effect as if amounts payable under confiscation orders were debts excepted under subsection (1)(a) of that section.

(2) In section 49(1)(g) of the Land Registration Act 1925 (protection of certain interests by notice) after "Charging Orders Act 1979" there is inserted "or the Drug Trafficking Offences Act 1986".

(3) In section 1(2)(a) of the Rehabilitation of Offenders Act 1974 (failure to pay fines etc. not to prevent person becoming rehabilitated) the reference to a fine or other sum adjudged to be paid by or imposed on a conviction does not include a reference to an amount payable under a confiscation order.

(4) After subsection (4) of section 18 of the Civil Jurisdiction and Judgements Act 1982 there is inserted the following subsection:

"(4A) This section does not apply as respects the enforcement in Scotland of orders made by the High Court in England and Wales under or for the purposes of the Drug Trafficking Offences Act 1986."

(5) Section 281(4) of the Insolvency Act 1986 (discharge of bankrupt not to release him from liabilities in respect of fines, etc.) shall have effect as if the reference to a fine included a reference to a confiscation order.

(6) Section 55(2) of the Bankruptcy (Scotland) Act 1985 (discharge of debtor not to release him from liabilities in respect of fines etc.) shall have effect as if the reference to a fine included a reference to a confiscation order.

Short title, commencement and extent

40.—(1) This Act may be cited as the Drug Trafficking Offences Act 1986.

(2) This Act, except section 35 (which comes into force on the day on which this Act is passed), shall come into force on such day as the Secretary of State may by order made by statutory instrument appoint and different days may be appointed for different provisions and for different purposes.

(3) Subject to subsections (4) and (5) below, this Act extends to England and Wales only.

(4) This Act has effect in Scotland as follows:

(a)   sections 7(4), 8 (but not subsection (8) or (9)), 11, 12 and 30 (but not subsection (10), (11) or (12)) extend also to Scotland, but only as provided by sections 20 and 21 of this Act;

144

(b) section 7(3);
    section 8(8) and (9);
    section 13;
    sections 15 to 17;
    section 18(1);
    section 24(3)*(a)*;
    sections 27 to 29;
    section 30(10), (11) and (12);
    section 34;
    section 38, so far as relating to other provisions of this Act extending to Scotland;
    section 39(3), (4) and (6); and
    this section, so far as relating to other provisions of this Act extending to Scotland,
  extend also to Scotland;
(c) sections 20 to 23 extend to Scotland only.

(5) Section 34 extends also to Northern Ireland.

Note on commencement

The following sections came into force on 30 September 1986:

section 24—see paras. 33.01–04 and Appendix XVI;
section 34—see para. 11.12 and Appendix III.

The whole Act was in force by 12 January 1987 (S.I. 1986/2145) so far as England and Wales are concerned. For Scotland the relevant provisions came into force on 1 January 1987 (S.I. 1986/2266).

The Crown Court (Amendment) Rules 1986

(S.I. No. 2151 (L. 17))

Made - - - - -	*8th December 1986*
Laid before Parliament	*9th December 1986*
Coming into Operation	*30th December 1986*

1. These Rules may be cited as the Crown Court (Amendment) Rules 1986 and shall come into operation on 30th December 1986.

2. The Crown Court Rules 1982[1] shall be amended by the insertion after Rule 25 of the following Rules:

"Statements relating to drug trafficking

25A.—(1) Where, in any proceedings in respect of a drug trafficking offence, the prosecutor or the defendant proposes to tender to the Crown Court any statement or other document under section 3 of the Drug Trafficking Offences Act 1986 he shall give a copy thereof as soon as practicable to the defendant or the prosecutor, as the case may be, and to the appropriate officer of the Crown Court.

(2) The appropriate officer of the Crown Court shall notify the prosecutor and the defendant as to the time within which any such statement or other document is required by the Crown Court to be tendered.

(3) Any statement tendered to the Crown Court by the prosecutor under section 3(1)*(a)* of the said Act of 1986 shall include the following particulars, namely:

(a) the name of the defendant;

(b) the name of the person by whom the statement is tendered;

(c) if the statement is tendered after the defendant has been convicted, the date on which and the place where the relevant conviction occurred;

(d) such information known to the prosecutor as is relevant to the determination whether the defendant has benefited from drug trafficking and to the assessment of the value of his proceeds of drug trafficking, together with an indication (so far as is known) of the dates on which any relevant payments or rewards were received by the defendant and their values.

(4) Expressions used in this Rule have the same meanings as in the said Act of 1986.

Investigation into drug trafficking—discharge and variation of orders

25B.—(1) Where an order under section 27 of the Drug Trafficking Offences Act 1986 has been made, the person required to comply with it may apply in writing

---

1 S.I. 1982/1109, to which there are amendments not relevant to these Rules.

to the appropriate officer of the Crown Court for the order to be discharged or varied, and on hearing such an application a Circuit judge may discharge the order or make such variations to it as he thinks fit.

(2) Subject to paragraph (3) below, where a person proposes to make an application under paragraph (1) above for the discharge or variation of an order, he shall give a copy of the application, not later than 48 hours before the making of the application, to a constable at the police station from which the application for the order was made, together with a notice indicating the time and place at which the application for discharge or variation is to be made.

(3) A Circuit judge may direct that paragraph (2) above need not be complied with if he is satisfied that the person making the application has good reason to seek a discharge or variation of the order as soon as possible and it is not practicable to comply with that paragraph.

(4) In this Rule:

"constable" includes a person commissioned by the Commissioners of Customs and Excise;
"police station" includes a place for the time being occupied by Her Majesty's Customs and Excise.".

Act of Adjournal (Drug Trafficking) 1986

(S.I. No. 2184 (S. 162))

Made - - - - -   *9th December 1986*
Coming into Operation   *1st January 1987*

Citations and commencement

1.—(1) This Act of Adjournal may be cited as the Act of Adjournal (Drug Trafficking) 1986 and shall come into operation on 1st January 1987.

(2) This Act of Adjournal shall be inserted in the Books of Adjournal.

Order to make material available

2.—(1) An application by the procurator fiscal to the sheriff for an order under section 27(2) of the Act of 1986[2] shall be made by way of petition; and section 310 of the Act of 1975[3] (incidental applications) shall apply to any such application as it applies to an application referred to in that section.

(2) The sheriff may make the order sought in the petition under sub-paragraph (1) before intimation of the petition to the person who appears to him to be in possession of the material to which the application relates.

(3) An application by the procurator fiscal for an order under section 27(5) of

2 The Drug Trafficking Offences Act 1986.
3 Criminal Procedure (Scotland) Act 1975, as amended by the Criminal Justice (Scotland) Act 1980 Sch. 7, para. 53 and Sch. 8.

147

the Act of 1986 (entry) may be made in the petition applying for an order under section 27(2); and sub-paragraph (2) applies to an order in respect of a person who appears to the sheriff to be entitled to grant entry to the premises in question as it applies to an order in respect of the person mentioned in that sub-paragraph.

Discharge and variation

3.—(1) A person, in respect of whom an order has been made under said section 27(2) or (5), may apply to the sheriff for discharge or variation of the order in question.

(2) The sheriff may, after hearing the parties, either grant or refuse to grant the discharge or variation sought.

Warrant to search premises

4.—An application by the procurator fiscal to the sheriff under section 28(1) of the Act of 1986 (authority for search) for a warrant authorising the search of specified premises may be made by way of petition; and section 310 of the Act of 1975 (incidental applications) shall apply to any such application for a warrant as it applies to an application for a warrant referred to in that section.

Rules of the Supreme Court, Order 115

(DRUG TRAFFICKING OFFENCES ACT 1986)

(This Order was added by R.S.C. (Amendment No. 3) 1986 (S.I. 1986/2289.)

Interpretation

1.—(1) In this Order "the Act" means the Drug Trafficking Offences Act 1986 and a section referred to by a number means the section so numbered in the Act.

(2) Expressions used in this Order which are used in the Act have the same meanings in this Order as in the Act.

Assignment of proceedings

2. The jurisdiction of the High Court under the Act shall be exercised by a judge of the Chancery Division or of the Queen's Bench Division in chambers.

Application for restraint order or charging order

3.—(1) An application for a restraint order under section 8 or for a charging order under section 9 (to either of which may be joined an application for the appointment of a receiver) may be made by the prosecutor ex parte or by originating motion.

(2) An application under paragraph (1) shall be supported by an affidavit, which shall:

(a) state the ground for believing that the defendant has benefitted from drug trafficking;

(b) state, as the case may be, either that the proceedings have been instituted against the defendant for a drug trafficking offence (giving particulars of the offence) and that they have not been concluded or that an information is to be laid that the defendant has or is suspected of having committed a drug trafficking offence;

(c) to the best of the deponent's ability, give full particulars of the realisable property in respect of which the order is sought and specify the person or persons holding such property;

(d) where proceedings have not been instituted, verify that the prosecutor is to have the conduct of the proposed proceedings;

(e) where proceedings have not been instituted, indicate when it is intended that they should be instituted.

(3) An originating motion under paragraph (1) shall be entitled in the matter of the defendant, naming him, and in the matter of the Act, and all subsequent documents in the matter shall be so entitled.

(4) Unless the court otherwise directs, and affidavit under paragraph (2) may contain statements of information or belief with the sources and grounds thereof.

Restraint order and charging order

4.—(1) A restraint order may be made subject to conditions and exceptions including but not limited to conditions relating to the indemnifying of third parties against expenses incurred in complying with the order, and expenses relating to living expenses and legal expenses of the defendant, but the plaintiff shall not be required to give an undertaking to abide by any order as to damages sustained by the defendant as a result of the restraint order.

(2) Unless the court otherwise directs, a restraint order made ex parte shall have effect until a day which shall be fixed for the hearing inter partes of the application and a charging order shall be an order to show cause, imposing the charge until such day.

(3) Where a restraint order is made the prosecutor shall serve copies of the order and of the affidavit in support on the defendant and on all other named persons restrained by the order and shall notify all other persons or bodies affected by the order or its terms.

(4) Where a charging order is made the prosecutor shall, unless the court otherwise directs, serve copies of the order and of the affidavit in support on the defendant and, where property to which the order relates is held by another person, on that person and shall serve a copy of the order on such of the persons or bodies specified in Order 50, rule 2(1)*(b)* to *(d)* as shall be appropriate.

Discharge or variation of order

5.—(1) Any person or body on whom a restraint order or a charging order is served or who is notified of such an order may apply by a summons to discharge or vary the order.

(2) The summons and the affidavit in support shall be lodged with the court and served on the prosecutor and, where he is not the applicant, on the defendant, not less than two clear days before the date fixed for the hearing of the summons.

(3) Upon the court being notified that proceedings for the offences have been concluded, or that the amount payment of which is secured by a charging order has been paid into court, any restraint order or charging order, as the case may be, shall be discharged.

Further application by prosecutor

6.—(1) Where a restraint order or charging order has been made the prosecutor may apply by summons or, where the case is one of urgency, ex parte:

(a) to discharge or vary such order, or
(b) for a restraint order or charging order in respect of other realisable property, or
(c) for the appointment of a receiver.

(2) An application under paragraph (1) shall be supported by an affidavit which, where the application is for a restraint order or a charging order, shall to the best of the deponent's ability give full particulars of the realisable property in respect of which the order is sought and specify the person or persons holding such property.

(3) The summons and affidavit in support shall be lodged with the court and served on the defendant and, where one has been appointed in the matter, on the receiver, not less than two clear days before the date fixed for the hearing of the summons.

(4) Rule 4(3) and (4) shall apply to the service of restraint orders and charging orders respectively made under this rule on persons other than the defendant.

Realisation of property

7.—(1) An application by the prosecutor under section 11 shall, where there have been proceedings against the defendant in the High Court, be made by summons and shall otherwise be made by originating motion.

(2) The summons or originating motion, as the case may be, shall be served with the evidence in support thereof not less than 7 days before the date fixed for the hearing of the summons on:

(a) the defendant;
(b) any person holding any interest in the realisable property to which the application relates; and
(c) the receiver, where one has been appointed in the matter.

(3) The application shall be supported by an affidavit, which shall, to the best of the deponent's ability, give full particulars of the realisable property to which it relates and specify the person or persons holding such property, and a copy of the confiscation order, of any certificate issued by the Crown Court under section 4(2) and of any charging order made in the matter shall be exhibited to such affidavit.

(4) The court may, on an application under section 11, exercise the power conferred by section 12(1) to direct the making of payments by the receiver.

Receivers

8.—(1) Subject to the provisions of this rule, the provisions of Order 30, rules 2 to 8 shall apply where a receiver is appointed in pursuance of a charging order or under section 8 or 11.

(2) Where the receiver proposed to be appointed has been appointed receiver in other proceedings under the Act, it shall not be necessary for an affidavit of fitness to be sworn or for the receiver to give security, unless the court otherwise orders.

(3) Where a receiver has fully paid the amount payable under the confiscation order and any sums remain in his hands, he shall apply by summons for directions as to the distribution of such sums.

(4) A summons under paragraph (3) shall be served with any evidence in support not less than 7 days before the date fixed for the hearing of the summons on:

(a) the defendant; and
(b) any other person who held property realised by the receiver.

Certificate of inadequacy

9.—(1) The defendant may apply by summons for a certificate under section 14(1).

(2) A summons under paragraph (1) shall be served with any supporting evidence not less than 7 days before the date fixed for the hearing of the summons on the prosecutor and on the receiver, where one has been appointed in the matter.

Compensation

10.—An application for an order under section 19 shall be made by summons, which shall be served, with any supporting evidence, on the person alleged to be in default and on the relevant authority under section 19(4) not less than 7 days before the date fixed for the hearing of the summons.

Disclosure of information

11.—(1) An application by the prosecutor under section 30 shall be made by summons, which shall state the nature of the order sought and whether material sought to be disclosed is to be disclosed to a receiver appointed under section 8 or 11 or in pursuance of a charging order or to a person mentioned in section 30(8).

(2) The summons and affidavit in support shall be served on the authorised Government Department in accordance with Order 77, rule 4 not less than 7 days before the date fixed for the hearing of the summons.

(3) The affidavit in support of an application under paragraph (1) shall state the grounds for believing that the conditions in section 30(4) and, if appropriate, section 30(7) are fulfilled.